Maria Edgew

Helen Zimmern

Alpha Editions

This edition published in 2022

ISBN : 9789356786332

Design and Setting By
Alpha Editions
www.alphaedis.com
Email - info@alphaedis.com

Contents

PREFACE.

THOUGH many notices of Miss Edgeworth have appeared from time to time, nothing approaching to a Life of her has been published in this country. As I have had the good fortune to have access to an unpublished memoir of her, written by her stepmother, as well as to a large number of her private letters, I am enabled to place what I hope is at least an authentic biography before the reader. Besides much kindness received from the members of Miss Edgeworth's family, I have also to acknowledge my obligations for help afforded in the preparation of this little book to Mrs. George Ticknor and Miss Ticknor of Boston, U. S. A., Mrs. Le Breton, Sir Henry Holland, Bart., the Rev. Canon Holland, the Rev. Dr. Sadler and Mr. F. Y. Edgeworth.

H. Z.

LONDON, August, 1883.

CHAPTER I.

INTRODUCTORY.

TOO many memoirs begin with tradition; to trace a subject *ab ovo* seems to have a fatal attraction for the human mind. It is not needful to retrace so far in speaking of Miss Edgeworth; but, for a right understanding of her life and social position, it is necessary to say some words about her ancestry. Of her family and descent she might well be proud, if ancestry alone, apart from the question whether those ancestors of themselves merit the admiration of their descendants, be a legitimate source of pride. The Edgeworths, originally established, it is believed, at Edgeworth, now Edgeware, in Middlesex, would appear to have settled in Ireland in the sixteenth century. The earliest of whom we have historical record is Roger Edgeworth, a monk, who followed in the footsteps of his sovereign, Henry VIII., both by being a defender of the faith and by succumbing to the bright eyes of beauty, for whose sake he finally renounced Catholicism and married. His sons, Edward and Francis; went to Ireland. The elder brother, Edward, became Bishop of Down and Connor, and died without issue. It was the younger, Francis, who founded the house of Edgeworth of Edgeworthstown; and ever since Edgeworthstown, in the county of Longford, Ireland, has remained in the possession of the family whence it derived its name. The Edgeworths soon became one of the most powerful families in the district, and experienced their full share of the perils and vicissitudes of the stormy period that apparently ended with the victories of William III. Most members of the family seem to have been gay and extravagant, living in alternate affluence and distress, and several of Maria Edgeworth's characters of Irish squires are derived from her ancestors. The family continued Protestant—the famous Abbé Edgeworth was a convert—and Maria Edgeworth's great-grandfather was so zealous in the reformed cause as to earn for himself the sobriquet of "Protestant Frank." His son married a Welsh lady, who became the mother of Richard Lovell Edgeworth, a man who will always be remembered as the father of his daughter. He was, however, something more than this; and as the lives of the father and daughter were throughout so intimately interwoven, a brief account of his career is needful for a comprehension of hers.

Richard Lovell Edgeworth was born at Bath in 1744, and spent his early years partly in England, partly in Ireland, receiving a careful education. In his youth he was known as "a gay philosopher," in the days when the word philosopher was still used in its true sense of a lover of wisdom. Light-hearted and gay, good-humored and self-complacent; possessed of an active and cultivated mind, just and fearless, but troubled with neither loftiness nor depth of feeling, Richard Lovell Edgeworth was nevertheless a remarkable personage, when the time at which he lived is taken into account. He foresaw much of the progress our own century has made, clearly indicated some of its features, and actually achieved for agriculture and industry a multitude of inventions, modest as far as the glory of the world attaches to them, but none the less useful for the services they render. Many of his ideas, rejected as visionary and impracticable when he first promulgated them, have now become the common property of mankind. He was no mere theorist; when he had established a theory he loved to put it into practice, and as his theories ranged over many and wide fields, so did his experiments. Even in late life, when most persons care only to cultivate repose, he threw himself, with all the ardor of youth, into schemes of improvement for the good of Ireland; for he was sincerely devoted to her true welfare, and held in contempt the mock patriotism that looks only to popularity. In early life he sowed a certain quantity of wild oats, the result of the super-abundant animal spirits that distinguished him, and at the age of sixteen contracted a mock-marriage, which his father found needful to have annulled by a process of law. After this escapade he was entered at Corpus Christi, Oxford, as a gentleman commoner. During his residence he became intimate with the family of Mr. Elers, a gentleman of German descent, who resided at Black Bourton, and was father to several pretty girls. Mr. Elers had previously warned the elder Edgeworth against introducing into his home circle the gay and gallant Richard, remarking that he could give his daughters no fortunes that would make them suitable matches for this young gentleman. Mr. Edgeworth, however, turned a deaf ear to the warning, and the result was that the collegian became so intimate at the house, and in time so entangled by the court he had paid to one of the daughters, that, although he had meanwhile seen women he liked better, he could not honorably extricate himself. In later life he playfully said: "Nothing but a lady ever did turn me aside from my duty." He certainly was all his days peculiarly susceptible to female charms, and, had opportunity been afforded him, might have rivalled Henry VIII. in the number of his wives. This second marriage gave as little satisfaction to his father as the first, but the elder Edgeworth wisely recognized the fact that he was himself not wholly blameless in the matter. He, therefore, a few months after the ceremony had been performed at Gretna Green, gave his consent to a formal re-marriage by license. Thus, before he was twenty, Richard Lovell Edgeworth was a husband and a father. The marriage entered upon so hastily proved unfortunate; the pair were totally unsuited to one another; and though Mrs. Edgeworth appears to have been a worthy woman, to judge from the few and somewhat ungenerous allusions her husband makes to her in his biography, they did not sympathize intellectually—a point he might have discovered before marriage. The consequence was that he sought sympathy and pleasure elsewhere. He divided his time between Ireland, London and Lichfield. The latter city was the centre of a somewhat prim, self-conscious, exclusive literary coterie, in which Dr. Darwin, the singer of the *Botanic Garden*, Miss Anna Seward, the "Swan of Lichfield," and the eccentric wife-trainer, Thomas Day, the author of *Sanford and Merton*, were conspicuous figures. They were most of them still in their youthful hey-day, unknown to fame, and, as yet, scarcely aspiring towards it. Here, in this, to him, congenial circle of eager and ardent young spirits, Richard Lovell Edgeworth loved to disport himself; now finding a sympathetic observer of his mechanical inventions in Mr. Watt, Dr. Darwin or Mr. Wedgwood; now flirting with the fair Anna. He must have posed as a bachelor, for he relates how, on one occasion, when paying compliments to Miss Seward, Mrs. Darwin took the opportunity of drinking "Mrs. Edgeworth's health," a name that caused manifest surprise to the object of his affections. Here, too, he became imbued with the educational theories of Rousseau, which clung to him, in a modified degree, throughout his life, and according to which, in their most pronounced form, he educated his eldest son. Here, further, at the age of twenty-six, he met the woman he was to love most deeply. From the moment he saw Miss Honora Sneyd, Mr. Edgeworth became enamored, and in his attentions to her he does not seem to have borne in mind the fact that he was a married man.

"I am not a man of prejudices," he complacently wrote in later life; "I have had four wives.[1] The second and third were sisters, and I was in love with the second in the life-time of the first."

The man who could make this public statement, and who could, moreover, leave to his daughter the task of publishing the record of his ill-assorted union with the woman who was her mother, was certainly one in whom good taste and good feeling were not preëminent. The birth of this daughter, who was destined to be his companion and friend, is an event he does not even note in his memoirs, which are more occupied with his affection for Miss Sneyd, from whose fascinations he at last felt it would be prudent to break away. He left England for a lengthened stay in France, taking with him his son, whose Rousseau education was to be continued, and accompanied by Mr. Day, who, to please Miss Elizabeth Sneyd, was about to put himself through a course of dancing and deportment, with a view to winning her consent to a marriage if he could succeed in taming his savage limbs and ideas into proper social decorum. The death of his wife recalled Mr. Edgeworth to England. With all possible speed he hastened to Lichfield, proposed to Honora Sneyd, was accepted, and married her within four months of his wife's demise. Mr. Edgeworth, the elder, had died some time previously; the son was now, therefore, master of Edgeworthstown. Immediately after his marriage he set out for Ireland, taking with him his bride and four little children. From that date forward a new era in his life commenced. It was not to run any longer in a separate course from that of his family.

CHAPTER II.

EARLY YEARS.

MARIA EDGEWORTH was born january 1st, 1767, in the house of her grandfather, Mr. Elers. Thus this distinguished authoress was an Englishwoman by birth, though Irish and German by race. At Black Bourton her earliest years were spent. Her father, who had taken in hand his little son to train according to the principles enunciated in *Emile*, took little notice of her, leaving her to the care of a fond, soft-hearted mother and doting aunts. The result was that the vivacity of her early wit was encouraged and the sallies of her quick temper unrepressed. Of her mother she retained little remembrance beyond her death, and how she was taken into the room to receive her last kiss. Mrs. Edgeworth had died in London at the house of some aunts in Great Russell street, and there Maria remained until her father's second marriage. Of her new mother Maria at first felt great awe, which soon gave place to sincere regard and admiration. Her father had been to her from babyhood the embodiment of perfection, and the mere fact that he required love from her for his new wife was sufficient to insure it. But she also learnt to love her for her own sake, and, indeed, if the statement of so partial a witness as Mr. Edgeworth can be accepted, she must have been a woman of uncommon power and charm.

Of her first visit to Ireland Maria recollected little except that she was a mischievous child. One day, when no one heeded her, she amused herself with cutting out the squares in a checked sofa-cover. Another day she trampled through a number of hot-bed frames that had just been glazed and laid on the grass. She could recall her delight at the crashing of the glass; but most immorally, and in direct opposition to her later doctrines, did not remember either cutting her feet or being punished for this freak. It was probably her exuberant spirits, added to the fact that Mrs. Honora Edgeworth's health began to fail after her removal to the damp climate of Ireland, that caused Maria to be sent to school. In 1775 she was placed at Derby with a Mrs. Latffiere, of whom she always spoke with gratitude and affection. Though eight years old, she would seem to have known very little, for she was wont to record that on the first day of her entrance into the school she felt more admiration at a child younger than herself repeating the nine parts of speech, than she ever felt afterwards for any effort of human genius. The first letter extant from her pen is dated thence, and though of no intrinsic merit, but rather the ordinary formal letter of a child under such circumstances, it deserves quotation because it is the first.

DERBY, March 30, 1776.

DEAR MAMMA:

It is with the greatest pleasure I write to you, as I flatter myself it will make you happy to hear from me. I hope you and my dear papa are well. School now seems agreeable to me. I have begun French and dancing, and intend to make ["great" was written, but a line was drawn through it] improvement in everything I learn. I know that it will give you great satisfaction to hear that I am a good girl. My cousin Clay sends her love to you; mine to father and sisters, who I hope are well. Pray give my duty to papa, and accept the same from, dear mamma,

YOUR DUTIFUL DAUGHTER.

It was at Derby that Maria learnt to write the clear, neat hand that never altered to the end of her life; and here too she acquired her proficiency in embroidery, an art she also practiced with success. As her parents shortly after came to reside in England for the benefit of Mrs. Edgeworth's health, Maria spent her holidays with them. Her stepmother appears to have taken great pains with her, conversing with her as an equal in every respect but age.

Her father had already commenced with her his system of educating the powers of the young mind by analytical reflection. He soon saw that hers was of no ordinary capacity. In 1780 he writes to her:—

It would be very agreeable to me, my dear Maria, to have letters from you FAMILIARLY: I wish to know what you like and what you dislike; I wish to communicate to you what little knowledge I have acquired, that you may have a tincture of every species of literature, and form your taste by choice and not by chance. Adieu! enjoy the pleasure of increasing the love and esteem of your excellent mother and of your

Affectionate Father.

Your poor mother continues extremely ill.

Less than a month afterwards Mr. Edgeworth had to announce the death of his wife. The letter in which he does so throws light on the relationship of father, daughter and stepmother:—

MY DEAR DAUGHTER:

At six o'clock on Thursday morning your excellent mother expired in my arms. She now lies dead beside me, and I know I am doing what would give her pleasure if she were capable of feeling anything, by writing to you at this time to fix her excellent image in your mind.

As you grow older and become acquainted with more of my friends, you will hear from every mouth the most exalted character of your incomparable mother. You will be convinced, by your own reflections upon her conduct, that she fulfilled the part of a mother towards you and towards your sisters, without partiality for her own or servile indulgence towards mine. Her heart, conscious of rectitude, was above the fear of raising suspicions to her disadvantage in the mind of your father or in the minds of other relatives. And though her timely restraint of you, and that steadiness of behavior, yielding fondness towards you only by the exact measure of your conduct, at first alarmed those who did not know her, yet now, my dearest daughter, every person who has the least connection with my family is anxious to give sincere testimony to their admiration of those very circumstances which they had too hastily, and from a common and well-grounded opinion, associated with the idea of a second wife.

Continue, my dear daughter, the desire which you feel of becoming amiable, prudent and of USE. The ornamental parts of a character with such an understanding as yours necessarily ensue; but true judgment and sagacity in the choice of friends, and the regulation of your behavior, can be had only from reflection and from being thoroughly convinced of what experience teaches, in general too late, that to be happy we must be good.

God bless you and make you ambitious of that valuable praise which the amiable character of your dear mother forces from the virtuous and the wise. My writing to you in my present situation will, my dearest daughter, be remembered by you as the strongest proof of the love of

Your Approving and Affectionate Father.

This letter, written at such a time, conveyed the impression intended, and thenceforward, even more than previously, the will to act up to the high opinion her father had formed of her character constituted the key-note of Maria Edgeworth's life, the exciting and controlling power.

At school as well as at home Maria distinguished herself as an entertaining story-teller. She soon learnt, with all the tact of an *improvisatrice*, to know which tale was most successful. Many of these were taken from books, but most were original. While entertaining her companions Maria studied their characters. It was at school she developed her keen penetration into the motives that sway actions. Here also she saw numbers, though on a small scale, and could estimate the effect of the voice on the multitude and the ease with which a mass can be governed. Very early indeed her father encouraged her to put her imaginings on paper; a remarkable proof of his enlightenment, for those were the days when female authorship was held in slight esteem, when for a woman to use her pen was regarded as a dangerous stepping beyond her boundary, which exposed her to suspicion and aversion. Soon after Mrs. Honora Edgeworth's death Mr. Edgeworth wrote:—

I also beg that you will send me a tale, about the length of a *Spectator*, upon the subject of GENEROSITY. It must be taken from history or romance, and must be sent the day se'nnight after you receive this, and I beg you will take some pains about it.

The same subject was given to a lad at Oxford, and Mr. Sneyd was chosen as umpire. He pronounced Maria's far the best. "An excellent story," he said, "and extremely well written, but where is the generosity?"—a saying which became a household proverb. This first story is not preserved, but Miss Edgeworth used to say that there was in it a sentence of inextricable confusion between a saddle, a man and his horse.

The same year Maria was removed from her unpretentious school to a fashionable establishment in London. Here she was to learn deportment and the showy accomplishments that in those days constituted the chief branches of a young lady's education. She was duly tortured on blackboards, pinioned in iron collars, made to use dumb-bells, and some rather stringent measures were taken to draw out her muscles and increase her stature. In vain; by nature she was a small woman, and small she remained. She also learnt to dance with grace in the days when dancing was something more dignified than a tearing romp, but music she failed in utterly. She had no taste for this art, and her music master, with a wisdom unhappily too rare, advised her to abandon the attempt to learn. She had been so well grounded in French and Italian, that when she came to do the exercises set her, she found them so easy that she wrote out at once those intended for the whole quarter, keeping them strung together in her desk, and unstringing them as required. The spare time thus secured was employed in reading for her own pleasure. Her favorite seat during play-time was under a cabinet which stood in the school-room, and here she often remained so absorbed in her book as to be deaf to all uproar. This early habit of concentrated attention was to stand her in good stead through life.

While his daughter was thus acquiring culture, Mr. Edgeworth was once more engaged in courtship. Mrs. Honora Edgeworth, recognizing her husband's nature, had recommended him on her death-bed to marry her sister Elizabeth, whose proposed marriage to Mr. Day had long ago fallen through. Though neither Elizabeth nor Mr. Edgeworth thought themselves suited to one another, Honora's advice prevailed, and within eight months after his last wife's death Mr. Edgeworth was once more married. It does not appear what Maria, now old enough to judge, thought of this new marriage, contracted so precipitately after the loss of one to whom Mr. Edgeworth was so devoted; but she doubtless held it right, as she held all done by her father, and she became to her new mother a warm and helpful friend.

Soon after this marriage Maria's eyes grew inflamed, and a leading physician pronounced in her hearing that she would infallibly lose her sight. The physical and mental sufferings hereby induced were keen, but they were borne with fortitude and patience. The summer holidays were spent as she had spent some previous ones—at Mr. Day's. This eccentric person had at last found a wife to his mind, and was settled in Surrey. The contrast between the mental atmosphere of her school, where externals were chiefly considered, and that at Mr. Day's, where these were scorned, did not fail to exercise an influence. She was deeply attached to her host, whose lofty mind and romantic character she honored. His metaphysical inquiries carried her into another world. Forbidden to use her eyes too much, she learnt in conversation with him. The icy strength of his system came at the right moment for annealing her principles, his severe reasoning and uncompromising love of truth awakened her powers, and the questions he put to her, the necessity of perfect accuracy in her answers, suited the bent of her mind. Though such strictness was not always agreeable, she even then perceived its advantages, and in after-life was deeply grateful to Mr. Day. The direction he gave her studies influenced her, as his friendship had in earlier days influenced her father. Mr. Day further plied her with tar-water, then deemed a sovereign remedy for all complaints. Either owing to this or the change of air, her eyes certainly grew better and her general health improved, although she remained delicate, subject to headaches, and unequal to much bodily exertion.

The following year (1782) her father resolved to return to Ireland to reside. He had seen on his brief visits the mischievous results of absenteeism, and felt that if it were in the power of any man to serve the country which gave him bread, he ought to sacrifice every inferior consideration and reside where he could be most useful. As, however, Mrs. Honora Edgeworth's health could not be pronounced an "inferior consideration," Mr. Edgeworth had been forced to live in England. Now, though his new wife had even before marriage shown consumptive symptoms, her constitution had so much strengthened that it seemed possible to inhabit the family house. Mr. Edgeworth therefore returned to Ireland with a firm determination to dedicate the remainder of his life to the education of his children, the improvement of his estate, and the endeavor to contribute to the amelioration of its inhabitants. He took Maria with him, and there now began for her the tranquil current of existence that was diversified by no remarkable events outside the domain of friendship and kindred. The home she now entered, the social and domestic duties she now undertook, continued the same for life. Her return to Ireland marks an epoch in her history.

CHAPTER III.

GIRLHOOD.

IRELAND is not among those countries that arouse in the hearts of strangers a desire to pitch their tents, and to judge from the readiness with which her own children leave her, we cannot suppose that they find her a fascinating land. And little wonder, when we consider the state of ferment and disorder which, in a greater or less degree, has always prevailed there. Yet Miss Edgeworth says:—

Things and persons are so much improved in Ireland of latter days, that only those who can remember how they were some thirty or forty years ago can conceive the variety of domestic grievances which, in those times, assailed the master of a family immediately upon his arrival at his Irish home. Wherever he turned his eyes, in or out of his house, damp, dilapidation, waste appeared. Painting, glazing, roofing, fencing, furnishing, all were wanting. The back yard, and even the front lawn round the windows of the house, were filled with loungers, "followers" and petitioners; tenants, under-tenants, drivers, sub-agent and agent, were to have audience; and they all had grievances and secret informations, accusations, reciprocating and quarrels each under each interminably. Alternately as landlord and magistrate, the proprietor of an estate had to listen to perpetual complaints, petty wranglings and equivocations, in which no human sagacity could discover the truth or award justice.

Returning to the country at the age of sixteen,[2] Maria Edgeworth looked at everything with fresh eyes. She was much struck with the difference between England and Ireland; the tones and looks, the melancholy and gaiety of the people, were new and extraordinary to her. A deep impression was made upon her observant mind, and she laid the foundations for those acute delineations of Irish character with which she afterwards delighted the world. It was her good fortune and ours that at an age when the mind is most impressionable she came into these novel scenes in lieu of having lived in their midst from childhood, when it is unlikely that she would so well have seized their salient traits.

It was June when the family arrived at Edgeworthstown, and though nominally summer, there was snow on the roses Maria ran out to gather. She felt as if transported into a novel and curious world. Unfortunately neither the situation nor the house of Edgeworthstown were beautiful; there was nothing here to arouse romance in the girl's nature. The country of Longford is in general flat, consisting of large districts of bog; only on the northern boundaries are there some remarkably sterile mountains. The house was an old-fashioned mansion, built with no pretensions to beauty. It needed much alteration and enlargement to suit the requirements of a growing family, and to accommodate his seven children suitably, Mr. Edgeworth saw himself forced to build. His extreme good sense guarded him from the usual errors committed by the Irish squires of that period, who were either content to live in wretched houses, out of repair, or to commence building on a scale as though they had the mines of Peru at their command, and then abandoning their plans as though they had not sixpence. The house at Edgeworthstown, without ever having pretensions to architecture, was simply made habitable. From the very commencement they began the even tenor of life that was to distinguish the family. The father was the centre of this remarkably united household. Miss Edgeworth says:—

Some men live with their family without letting them know their affairs; and, however great may be their affection and esteem for their wives and children, think that they have nothing to do with business. This was not my father's way of thinking. Whatever business he had to do was done in the midst of his family, usually in the common sitting-room, so that we were intimately acquainted, not only with his general principles of conduct, but with the most minute details of their every-day application. I further enjoyed some peculiar advantages: he kindly wished to give me habits of business; and for this purpose allowed me, during many years, to assist him in copying his letters of business, and in receiving his rents.

Indeed, from their arrival the eldest daughter was employed as her father's agent, for it was Mr. Edgeworth's conviction that to remedy some of the worst evils of his unhappy country, it was needful to get rid of the middle-men. On his own estate he was resolved not to let everything go wrong for the good old Irish reason that it had always been so. He labored with zeal, justice, forbearance. He received his rents direct, he chose his tenants for their character, he resisted sub-division of holdings, and showed no favor to creed or nationality. Miss Edgeworth proved herself his worthy daughter. She exhibited acuteness and patience in dealing with the tenants, admiring their talents while seeing their faults; generous, she was not to be duped; and just, she was not severe. Thus in a brief time, thanks to this firm but kindly government, their estate came to be one of the best managed in the county. The work it induced was certainly fortunate for Maria; besides teaching her habits of business, it made her familiar with the modes of thought and expression of the Irish. She learnt to know them thoroughly and truly at their best and at their worst.

But Maria's entire time was not occupied with the tenantry. It was a part of her father's system that young children should not be left to servants, from whom he deemed, not without justice, that they learnt much that was undesirable. He therefore committed to the charge of each of his elder girls one of their younger brothers and sisters, and little Henry, Mrs. Elizabeth Edgeworth's child, fell to Maria's lot. She devoted herself with ardor to the boy, and was fondly attached to him. But it was, of course, the father who superintended the general education, following the lines afterwards laid down in *Practical Education.* His system certainly succeeded with his numerous children, though it might, as a rule, incline to make the pupils somewhat presumptuous, self-sufficient and pragmatical. The animation spread through the house by connecting the children with all that was going on was highly useful; it awakened and excited mental exertion, and braced the young people to exercise independence of thought. Mr. Edgeworth made no empty boast when he wrote to Mr. Darwin:—

"I do not think one tear per month is shed in this house, nor the voice of reproof heard, nor the hand of restraint felt."

How primitive was the state of Ireland in those days can be gathered from the fact that, except bread and meat, all articles of food and household requirement were to be had only in Dublin, and not always even there. Neither was there much congenial society. The Edgeworths had no liking for the country gentlemen who spent their lives in shooting, hunting and carousing,—booby squires who did not even know that their position put duties upon them. Formal dinners and long sittings, with the smallest of small talk, were the order of the day and night. They were, however, fortunate in finding in this social wilderness some few persons really worth knowing, chief among whom were the families resident at Pakenham Hall and Castle Forbes. The former house, the residence of Lord Longford, was only twelve miles distant, but it was separated from Edgeworthstown by a vast bog, a bad road, an awkward ferry and an ugly country. Nevertheless, these obstacles were braved, and at Pakenham Hall Maria met many people of literary and political distinction. At Castle Forbes, some nine miles distant, by a more practicable road, there was also to be met society varied and agreeable, more especially so when Lady Granard's mother, Lady Moira, was in the country. Lady Moira was a woman of noble character, much conversational talent and general knowledge. As daughter to the Countess of Huntingdon she had seen much strange society, and had been in the very midst of the evangelical revival. Besides this she was a person of great influence in Ireland. Her house in Dublin was the resort of the wise and witty of the day, hence she was able to initiate Maria into a new and larger world, to expand her ideas, and to increase her insight into character. It was indeed fortunate for Miss Edgeworth that this old lady took a special fancy to her. She was in those days very reserved in manner and little inclined to converse—a contrast to after years, when her conversation delighted all listeners. It was, perhaps, partly weak health that made her silent, but probably yet more the consciousness of great powers which were under-rated or misunderstood by her youthful contemporaries. She had no frivolous small society talk to offer them. Lady Moira, however, recognized the capacity of this timid, plain, inoffensive young girl. She talked to her, drew her out, plied her with anecdotes of her own experiences in life, and gave her the benefit of her riper wisdom.

Thus Miss Edgeworth early lived with and learnt to understand the fashionable society of which she wrote so much. It is always fortunate for a novelist to be born, as she was, amid the advantages of refinement and breeding, without being elevated out of reach of the interests and pleasures which dwell in the middle ranks. For want of this, many, even amongst the most eminent writers of fiction, have suffered shipwreck.

While thus reserved in society, Maria relaxed with her father. She knew he appreciated her powers, and his approbation was sufficient at all times to satisfy her. One of her pleasures was to ride out with him—not that she was a good horsewoman, for she was constitutionally timid, but because it afforded her the opportunity of uninterrupted exchange of talk. It was on these rides that most of their writings were planned.

In the autumn of their return to Ireland (1782) Miss Edgeworth began, at her father's suggestion, to translate Madame de Genlis' *Adèle et Théodore*. It was her first work intended for publication. The appearance of Holcroft's translation prevented its execution, but neither she nor her father regarded the time bestowed on it as misspent; it gave her that readiness and choice of words which translation teaches. Mr. Day, who had a horror of female authorship, remonstrated with Mr. Edgeworth for having ever allowed his daughter to translate, and when he heard that the publication was prevented, wrote a congratulatory letter on the event. It was from the recollection of the arguments he used, and from her father's replies, that five years afterwards Miss Edgeworth wrote her *Letters to Literary Ladies*, though they were not published till after the death of Mr. Day. Indeed, it is possible that had he lived Maria Edgeworth would have remained unknown to fame, so great was her father's deference to his judgment, though sensible that there was much prejudice mixed with his reasons. "Yet," adds Miss Edgeworth, "though publication was out of our thoughts, as subjects occurred, many essays and tales were written for private amusement."

The first stories she wrote were some of those now in the *Parent's Assistant* and *Early Lessons*. She wrote them on a slate, read them out to her sisters and brothers, and, if they approved, copied them. Thus they were at once put to the test of childish criticism; and it is this, and living all her life among children, that has made Miss Edgeworth's children's stories so inimitable. She understood children, knew them, sympathized with them. Her father's large and ever-increasing family, in which there were children of all ages, gave her a wide and varied audience of youthful critics, among the severest in the world. Many of her longer tales and novels were also written or planned during these years. Her father had, however, imbued her with the Horatian maxim, *novumque prematur in annum*, so that many things lay by for years to be considered by her and her father, recorrected, revised, with the result that nothing was ever given to the world but the best she could produce.

Thus, contented, busy, useful, the even course of her girlhood flowed on and merged into early womanhood, with no more exciting breaks than the arrival of a box of new books from London, an occasional visit to her neighbors, or, best of all, to Black Castle, a few hours' drive from Edgeworthstown, where lived her father's favorite sister, Mrs. Ruxton, her aunt and life-long friend. For forty-two years aunt and niece carried on an uninterrupted correspondence, while their meetings were sources of never-failing delight.

In 1789 the sudden death of Mr. Day deprived Mr. Edgeworth of a valued friend. This man, who, for a person not actually insane, was certainly one of the oddest that ever walked this earth, with his mixture of *mauvaise honte* and savage pride, misanthropy and philanthropy, had exercised a great influence on both their lives. They felt his loss keenly. Another sorrow quickly followed. Honora, the only daughter of Mrs. Honora Edgeworth, a girl of fifteen, endowed with beauty and talents, fell a victim to the family disease. The next year Lovell, the now only surviving child of Honora, also showed signs of consumption. It became needful to remove him from Ireland, and Mr. and Mrs. Edgeworth therefore crossed to England, leaving Maria in charge of the other children. A house was taken at Clifton, and here Miss Edgeworth and her charges rejoined their parents. The conveying so large a party so long a journey in those days was no small undertaking for a young woman of twenty-four. The responsibility was terrible to her, though she afterwards dwelt only on the comic side. At one of the inns where they slept, the landlady's patience was so much tried by the number of little people getting out of the carriage and the quantity of luggage, that she exclaimed: "Haven't you brought the kitchen grate too?"

At Clifton the Edgeworths resided for two years. Miss Edgeworth writes to her Uncle Ruxton:—

We live just the same kind of life that we used to do at Edgeworthstown, and though we move amongst numbers, are not moved by them, but feel independent of them for our daily amusement. All the *phantasmas* I had conjured up to frighten myself vanished after I had been here a week, for I found that they were but phantoms of my imagination, as you very truly told me. We live very near the Downs, where we have almost every day charming walks, and all the children go bounding about over hill and dale along with us.

In a later letter she says that they are not quite as happy here as at home, but have a great choice of books which they enjoy. While at Clifton the eldest son visited them. His Rousseau education had turned him out an ungovernable child of nature; he neither could nor would learn, so there remained no alternative but to allow him to follow his inclinations, which happily led him towards nothing more mischievous than a sailor's life. At Clifton, too, they became acquainted with Dr. Beddoes, who soon after married Maria's sister Anna, and became the father of Thomas Lovell Beddoes, the poet of Death. A baby child also died within those two years, which thus embraced meetings, partings, courtships, much pleasant social intercourse, and much serious study. For Maria it also included a visit to an old school-fellow in London:—

She was exceeding kind to me, and I spent most of my time with her as I liked. I say most, because a good deal of it was spent in company, where I heard of nothing but chariots and horses, and curricles and tandems. Oh, to what contempt I exposed myself in a luckless hour, by asking what a tandem was! Since I have been away from home I have missed the society and fondness of my father, mother and sisters, more than I can express, and more than beforehand I could have thought possible; I long to see them all again. Even when I am most amused I feel a void, and now I understand what an aching void is perfectly well.

A letter written from Clifton is a charming specimen of Miss Edgeworth's easy, warm-hearted family missives, which, like most family letters, contain little of intrinsic value, and yet throw much light upon the nature of their writer:—

CLIFTON, Dec. 13, 1792.

The day of retribution is at hand, my dear aunt. The month of May will soon come, and then when we meet face to face, and voucher to voucher, it shall be truly seen whose letter-writing account stands fullest and fairest in the world. Till then "we'll leave it all to your honor's honor." But why does my dear aunt write, "I can have but little more time to spend with my brother in my life," as if she was an old woman of one hundred and ninety-nine and upwards? I remember the day I left Black Castle you told me, if you recollect, that "you had one foot in the grave;" and though I saw you standing before me in perfect health, sound wind and limb, I had the weakness to feel frightened, and never to think of examining where your feet really were. But in the month of May we hope to find them safe in your shoes, and I hope that the sun will then shine out, and that all the black clouds in the political horizon will be dispersed, and that "freemen" will, by that time, eat their puddings and hold their tongues. Anna and I stayed one week with Mrs. Powys, at Bath, and were very thoroughly occupied all the time with seeing and—I won't say with being seen; for though we were at three balls, I do not believe any one saw us. The upper rooms we thought very splendid and the play-houses pretty, but not so good as the theatre at Bristol. We walked all over Bath with my father, and liked it extremely: he showed us the house where he was born.

The day of retribution was indeed nearer at hand than she anticipated. In the autumn of 1793 the news of Irish disturbances grew so alarming that Mr. Edgeworth thought it his duty to return immediately. The caravan was therefore once more transported to Edgeworthstown.

CHAPTER IV.

WOMANHOOD.

ON their return the Edgeworths at first inclined to think that the English papers had exaggerated the Irish disturbances. Accustomed to a condition of permanent discontent, they were relieved to find that though there were alarms of outrages committed by "Hearts of Oak Boys" and "Defenders," though there were nightly marauders about Edgeworthstown, though Mr. Edgeworth had been threatened with assassination, still, all things considered, "things in their neighborhood were tolerably quiet." In this matter as in others, of course, the basis of comparison alone constitutes the value of the inference deduced. In any case the family resumed their quiet course of existence; Mr. Edgeworth busy with the invention of a telegraph, Miss Edgeworth writing, helping to educate the little ones, visiting and being visited by her Aunt Ruxton. In the evenings the family gathered round the fireside and the father read aloud. Late in 1793 Miss Edgeworth writes:—

This evening my father has been reading out Gay's *Trivia*, to our great entertainment. I wished very much, my dear aunt, that you and Sophy had been sitting round the fire with us. If you have *Trivia*, and if you have time, will you humor your niece so far as to look at it? I had much rather make a bargain with any one I loved to read the same book with them at the same hour, than to look at the moon like Rousseau's famous lovers. "Ah! that is because my dear niece has no taste and no eyes." But I assure you I am learning the use of my eyes main fast, and make no doubt, please Heaven I live to be sixty, to see as well as my neighbors. I am scratching away very hard at the *Freeman Family*.[3]

That Miss Edgeworth was not affected by the current sentimentalism of the period, the above remark shows. Indeed, her earliest letters evince her practical, straightforward common sense. Romance had no place in her nature. In 1794 she was engaged upon her *Letters to Literary Ladies*. She wrote to her cousin:—

Thank my aunt and thank yourself for kind inquiries after *Letters to Literary Ladies*. I am sorry to say they are not as well as can be expected, nor are they likely to mend at present; when they are fit to be seen—if that happy time ever arrives—their first visit shall be to Black Castle. They are now disfigured by all manner of crooked marks of papa's critical indignation, besides various abusive marginal notes, which I would not have you see for half-a-crown sterling, nor my aunt for a whole crown as pure as King Hiero's.

The arts of peace, as she herself expresses it, were going on prosperously side by side with those of war; the disturbances, of which Miss Edgeworth continues to write quite lightly, having become sufficiently serious to require military intervention.

In 1795 the *Letters to Literary Ladies* were published. Considering the time when the work was written it showed much independence and advance of thought, though to-day it would be stigmatized as somewhat retrograde. It is nothing more than a plea in favor of female education, repeating arguments that of late years have been well worn, and of which the world, for some time past convinced of the wisdom of according education to women, no longer stands in need. The book is interesting to-day merely as another proof of how much Mr. Edgeworth and his daughter were advanced in thought. They could not be brought to the common opinion then prevalent that ignorance was a woman's safeguard, that taste for literature was calculated to lead to ill conduct, though even a thinker so enlightened in many respects as Mr. Day indorsed Sir Anthony Absolute's dictum that the extent of a woman's erudition should consist in her knowing her letters, without their mischievous combinations.

Not even the honors of first authorship could cause Miss Edgeworth's private letters, then any more than afterwards, to be occupied with herself. "I beg, dear Sophy," she writes to her cousin, "that you will not call my little stories by the sublime title of 'my works;' I shall else be ashamed when the little mouse comes forth." It is the affairs of others, the things that it will please or amuse her correspondents to hear, that she writes about. The tone is always good-humored and kindly.

Ever and again the noiseless tenor of her way was disturbed by the insurgents. She writes, January, 1796:—

You, my dear aunt, who were so brave when the county of Meath was the seat of war, must know that we emulate your courage; and I assure you, in your own words, "that whilst our terrified neighbors see nightly visions of massacres, we sleep with our doors and windows unbarred." I must observe, though, that it is only those doors and windows that have neither bolts nor bars that we leave unbarred, and these are more at present than we wish even for the reputation of our valor. All that I crave for my own part is that if I am to have my throat cut, it may not be by a man with his face blackened with charcoal. I shall look at every person that comes here very closely, to see if there be any marks of charcoal upon their visages. Old wrinkled offenders, I should suppose, would never be able to wash out their stains, but in others a *very* clean face will, in my mind, be a strong symptom of guilt— clean hands proof positive, and clean nails ought to hang a man.

In 1796 appeared the first volume of the *Parent's Assistant*. It is agreeable to learn from a letter of hers that she was not responsible for this clumsy title:—

My father had sent the *Parent's Friend*, but Mr. Johnson has degraded it into *Parent's Assistant*, which I dislike particularly from association with an old book of arithmetic called the *Tutor's Assistant*.

The book was so successful that the publisher expressed a wish for more volumes, to be brought out with illustrations. Miss Beaufort, the daughter of a neighboring clergyman, was entrusted with the artistic commission, which led to an intimacy between the families. Meanwhile Miss Edgeworth, stimulated by success, continued to write new stories, and to correct and revise old ones. The *Moral Tales* were conceived at this time, and the idea of writing on Irish Bulls had occurred to her. She was also busy upon *Practical Education*. At the same time Mrs. Elizabeth Edgeworth's health, that had long been precarious, gave way, and in November, 1797, to the sorrow of all the circle, she fell a victim to consumption. As before, Mr. Edgeworth was soon consoled. It was in the direction of Miss Beaufort that he turned his eyes. There must certainly have been something attractive in this man, now past fifty, three times a widower, with a numerous family by different wives, that could induce a young girl to regard him as a wooer. Miss Edgeworth frankly owns that when she first knew of this attachment she did not wish for the marriage. But her father, with his persuasive tongue, overcame her objections.

Mr. Edgeworth himself announced his intending nuptials to Dr. Darwin, at the end of a long letter dealing with the upas tree, frogs, agriculture, hot-water pipes, and so forth:—

And now for my piece of news, which I have kept for the last: I am going to be married to a young lady of small fortune and large accomplishments—compared with my age, much youth (not quite 30) and more prudence—some beauty, more sense—uncommon talents, more uncommon temper—liked by my family, loved by me. If I can say all this three years hence, shall not I have been a fortunate, not to say a wise man?

He was able to say so not only three years after, but to the end of his life. Whatever may be thought of Mr. Edgeworth's many and hasty marriages, it must be admitted that they all turned out to the happiness of himself and his children. Miss Edgeworth wrote a long letter to her future stepmother, characteristic both of her amiable disposition, her filial piety and her method of regarding love. "Miss Edgeworth's Cupid," as Byron observed, "was always something of a Presbyterian." In it she assures Miss Beaufort (who was her junior) that she will find her "gratefully exact *en belle fille*;" a promise she fulfilled beyond the letter.

Within seven months of his late wife's death, just as public affairs were assuming a still stormier aspect, and the nation about to burst into the rebellion of 1798, Mr. Edgeworth was once more a bridegroom. The wedding trip of the couple took them through the disturbed districts; they beheld rebels hidden in the potato furrows, and passed a car between whose shafts the owner had been hanged—a victim to the "Defenders." But in the house of Edgeworthstown there was, as ever, peace and concord; and the trying situation upon which the new wife was called to enter was smoothed for her even by the children of the woman whom she had so quickly displaced in their father's affection.

In an incredibly short time all things and people found themselves in their proper places, and the new Mrs. Edgeworth soon proved herself a fitting person to hold the reins of household government. Only a month after the marriage Miss Edgeworth can tell her cousin:—

We are indeed happy. The more I see of my friend and mother, the more I love and esteem her, and the more I feel the truth of all that I have heard you say in her praise. So little change has been made in the way of living, that you would feel as if you were going on with your usual occupations and conversation amongst us. We laugh and talk and enjoy the good of every day, which is more than sufficient. How long this may last we cannot tell. I am going on in the old way, writing stories. I cannot be a captain of dragoons, and sitting with my hands before me would not make any of us one degree safer. I have finished a volume of wee-wee stories about the size of the *Purple Jar*, all about Rosamond. My father has made our little rooms so nice for us; they are all fresh painted and papered. Oh, rebels! oh, French! spare them. We have never injured you, and all we wish is to see everybody as happy as ourselves.

The summer passed with immunity from open insurrection in County Longford; but it shortly appeared that the people were secretly leagued with the rest of their countrymen, and only waited the arrival of the French to break into rebellion. Soon the whole district about Edgeworthstown was disturbed, and in September it was needful for the family to beat a precipitate retreat from home, leaving it in the hands of the rebels. Happily it was spared from pillage, thanks to one of the invaders, to whom Mr. Edgeworth had once shown kindness. The family were only away five days. A battle had speedily settled the rebels and dispersed the French, whom their own allies had deserted at the first volley. But those days, although only five days, seemed a life-time to Miss Edgeworth, from the dangers and anxieties the family underwent in their course.

By November all disturbances had so far subsided around Edgeworthstown as to allow the family to busy themselves with private theatricals, Miss Edgeworth writing the play, the children acting it, the father building the stage. At the end of the year Mr. Edgeworth was returned for the last Irish Parliament, and the family went with him to Dublin. The Union was then the hot theme of debate, the Irish having incontestably shown themselves incapable of home rule. Mr. Edgeworth very characteristically spoke for the Union and voted against it, declaring "that England has not any right to do Ireland good against her will."

In the spring of 1799 Mr., Mrs. and Miss Edgeworth went to England and renewed their acquaintance with Mr. Watt, Dr. Darwin and Mr. William Strutt of Derby. They also came into contact with many literary celebrities, Mr. Edgeworth now posing as an author upon the strength of *Practical Education*, written in partnership with his daughter, who was ever not only willing but anxious that he should bear off all the honor and glory. Among their acquaintance was Mrs. Barbauld, for whom both father and daughter conceived a genuine regard, and whom Mr. Edgeworth liked the more because she was a proof of the soundness of his belief that the cultivation of literary tastes does not necessarily unfit a woman for her domestic duties. In London they also visited their publisher, Mr. Johnson, an intelligent, generous, but most dilatory man, who was then confined in King's Bench Prison on account of some publication held treasonable. Of this English visit there are, unfortunately, only two letters preserved: one announcing the birth of another baby into this already huge family, the other treating of "a young man, Mr. Davy,[4] who has applied himself much to chemistry, has made some discoveries of importance, and enthusiastically expects wonders will be performed by the use of certain gases."

With the dissolution of the last Irish Parliament, Mr. Edgeworth's public duties came to an end, and the quiet, happy life at Edgeworthstown recommenced its even course, marked only by the publication of Miss Edgeworth's works, and by births and deaths in the family circle.

CHAPTER V.

"PRACTICAL EDUCATION."—CHILDREN'S BOOKS.

TWO circumstances must never be lost sight of in speaking of Miss Edgeworth's writings: the one, that she did not write from the inner prompting of genius, but rather because it had been suggested by her father; the other, that she wrote throughout with a purpose in view, and by no means only for the sake of affording amusement. To blame her, therefore, as has been so often done, for being utilitarian in her aim, is to blame her for having attained her goal. A minor consideration, but one that often proves of no minor weight, was the fact that Miss Edgeworth never needed to follow authorship as a profession; its pecuniary results were of no moment to her, and hence she was spared all the bitterness and incidental anxieties of an author's life, the working when the brain should rest, the imperative need to go on, no matter whether there be aught to say or not. Her path, in this respect, as in all others, traversed the high-roads of life. Fame at once succeeded effort; the heart-sickness of hope deferred was never hers; she was therefore neither soured nor embittered by feeling within herself powers which the world was unwilling or slow to acknowledge.

It was in 1798 that were published two large octavo volumes, called *Practical Education*, bearing upon the title-page the joint names of Richard Lovell and Maria Edgeworth. This was the first partnership work of father and daughter, that literary partnership "which for so many years," says Miss Edgeworth, "was the joy and pride of my life." The book was the outcome of a series of observations and facts relative to children, not originally intended for publication, registered first by Mr. Edgeworth and his wife Honora, and afterwards continued by Mrs. Elizabeth Edgeworth. In consequence of Mr. Edgeworth's exhortations, Miss Edgeworth also began in 1791 to note down anecdotes of the children around her, and to write out some of her father's conversation lessons. The reason for giving all this to the world was that though assertions and theories on education abounded, facts and experiments were wanting. Undaunted by the fear of ridicule or the imputation of egotism, Mr. Edgeworth bade his daughter work the raw materials into shape, blending with anecdotes and lessons the principles of education that were peculiarly his. For this work Miss Edgeworth claims for her father the merit of having been the first to recommend, both by practice and precept, what Bacon called the experimental method in education. Mr. Edgeworth, as we know, was a disciple of the crude, mechanical school of Rousseau; and though, owing to his failure with his eldest son, he had seen the necessity of some modification, he had never wholly abandoned it, and had imbued his daughter with the same ideas. Happily for her, however, her earliest training had been less rigid than that of her brothers and sisters. She thus obtained elbow-room for that development which her father's formal and overloading system might have crushed. But of this she was unconscious, and she was ready to echo his opinions, believe in them blindly and propagate them.

The book, though prolix, dull and prosy in part, containing much repetition, many paltry illustrations, many passages, such as the chapter on servants, that might be omitted with advantage, was, as a whole, of value, and would not even now be quite out of date. But its chief and abiding merit is that it was a step in the right direction; and its worth must on that account be emphasized, although this was exaggerated by Miss Edgeworth's filial fondness. There were in those days no text-books for the first principles of knowledge for the young; and though education had been a favorite theme with all the philosophers, from Aristotle to Locke, their systems were too remote for practical application. The inevitable but lamentable consequence was, that theories of education were disregarded just by those very persons who had the training of the young in their hands. They were pleased to sneer at them as metaphysics. So much space was given in works of this nature to speculation, so little to practical application of proved and admitted truths, that the mere word metaphysics sounded to the majority of readers as a name denoting something perplexing and profound, but useless as a whole. Yet, as Miss Edgeworth pertinently observed in her preface to *Harry and Lucy*, after being too much the fashion, metaphysics had been thrown aside too disdainfully, and their use and abuse confounded. Without an attentive examination of the operations of the mind, especially as developed at an early age, every attempt at systematic education is mere working at random. The great merit of Mr. and Miss Edgeworth's works may be stated in her own words:—

Surely it would be doing good service to bring into popular form all that metaphysicians have discovered which can be applied to practice in education. This was early and long my father's object. The art of teaching to invent—I dare not say, but of awakening and assisting the inventive power by daily exercise and excitement, and by the application of philosophic principles to trivial occurrences,—he believed might be pursued with infinite advantage to the rising generation.

The authors of *Practical Education* did not seek to appeal to grave and learned persons, like the former writers on these themes, but to the bulk of mankind, in whose hands, after all, lies their application. In this series of somewhat rambling essays, of the most miscellaneous description, there are no abstruse or learned disquisitions, there is nothing like a process of reasoning from beginning to end; it is essentially a treatise for the mass. On every page there are remarks for which previous authorities can be found; original ideas are rare; nevertheless the whole is expressed so lucidly and familiarly, the entire work is so crowded with illustrations of the simplest and most obvious kind, that "the unwary reader can easily be entrapped into the belief that he is perusing nothing more serious than a lively and agreeable essay upon the tempers and capacities of children, written by two good-natured persons who are fond of amusing themselves with young people." Mr. Edgeworth believed according to the proverb, "that youth and white paper can take all impressions," that everything could be achieved by education; that, given the individual, it was possible to make of him whatever the instructor pleased. Of course our present more scientific mode of thought, our superior scientific knowledge, shows us the untenability of so dogmatic a persuasion; but it was characteristic of the eighteenth century, forms the key-note to many of their educational experiments, and furnishes the reason of their failures. The times when Mr. Edgeworth wrote and devised his doctrines were "the good old days when George the Third was King," when education was at a discount, when to have a taste for literature was to be held a pedant or a prig. If Mr. Edgeworth went too far in his earnest advocacy of careful training for the young of both sexes, in his belief in the result, our modern school has perhaps, in the latter respect, erred on the other side. We know now that it is out of the power of education to change nature. Yet our scientific knowledge has inclined us, perhaps unduly, to under-rate the value of training, and to allow too much play to the doctrine of *laissez-faire*. As ever, the truth lies in the middle; and in any case, because we are at present going through a period of reaction, we should refrain from sneering at those perhaps over-earnest men, of whom Mr. Edgeworth was a type, who, in a frivolous age, rebelled against their unthinking contemporaries. It is too much the fashion to stigmatize these men as prigs; pragmatic no doubt they were, conceited and self-confident, and, like all minorities, over-ardent. Still it cannot be enough borne in mind that the people of that period who thought, thought more and read more thoroughly than those of to-day. They came to original conclusions; they did not imbibe so much at second-hand by means of criticism and ready-made opinions. Of this, Miss Edgeworth and her father were notable examples; to this, her letters bear abundant testimony.

In the preface to *Practical Education* the respective shares of father and daughter in the work are stated. He wrote all relating to the art of teaching in the chapter on tasks, grammar, classical literature, geography, chronology, arithmetic and mechanics; the rest, considerably more than half, was by her.

"The firm of Edgeworth & Co.," as Sydney Smith named them, had now attained literary notoriety. Their book, on its appearance, was praised and abused enough to render its authors speedily famous. Mr. Edgeworth, with his enormous family, had, of course, had good opportunities of observation and experiment in the domain of education. It was conceded that there was much that was wise and useful in his pages, mixed with much that was absurd and dogmatic. But the real life and animation for his tenets was to come from his daughter, who was to carry them further than they would undoubtedly otherwise have gone, and the fact that quite two generations of English men and women were instilled into Edgeworthian doctrines is due entirely and alone to her. She made it the business of her life to illustrate the pedantic maxims of her father, and it has been ably remarked that between these narrow banks her genius flowed through many and diverse volumes of amusing tales. It was with this aim in view that *The Parent's Assistant, Harry and Lucy, Frank and Rosamond*, and *Early Lessons*, those companions of the nursery, were penned. Though not all published at this time—the continuation of *Harry and Lucy* not, indeed, until many years later—it is convenient to treat of them all together, as they are one in unity of thought and design.

Fully to estimate what Miss Edgeworth did for the children of her time, and that immediately succeeding it, it is needful to point out the wide contrast between those days and ours. To-day the best authors do not think it beneath their dignity to write for children—quite otherwise; while formerly few persons of any literary ability condescended to write children's books. In those days, therefore, nursery libraries were not, as now, richly stocked, and children either did not read at all, or, if they were of a reading disposition, read the works intended for their elders, often, it must be admitted, with the good result that a solid foundation of knowledge of the English classics was laid. Still it was only exceptional children who attempted these tougher tasks; most either did not read at all or read such poor literature as was at hand. In a series of able articles published some years ago, Miss Yonge has traced the history of children's books. For a long time there were no such things; then came some tales translated from the French and judiciously trimmed, besides a few original stories of more or less merit, to which latter category belonged *Goody Two-Shoes*. This was followed by the reign of didactic works which began with Mrs. Trimmer, whose original impulse came from Rousseau. It was his *Emile* that had aroused the school which produced Madame de Genlis in France, Campe in Germany, and in England the Aikens, Hannah More, the Taylors of Norwich, and Mr. Day. It was a famine that had to be met, and much stodgy food was devoured, many long, hard words were laboriously spelt out, the pabulum offered was but too often dull and dreary. Realism had invaded the nursery, strong, high purpose was the first aim in view, and entertainment was held a secondary consideration. As for the poor dear fairies, they had been placed under a ban by the followers of Jean Jacques. Fairy tales were treated as the novels of childhood, and held by this school to cultivate the heart and imagination unduly, and to arouse disgust with the assigned lot in life, which is rarely romantic, but consists rather of common-place pleasure and pain.

The Edgeworths' ambition was to write the history of realities in an entertaining manner; they held that it was better for purposes of education, and more suited to the tastes of children, than improbable fiction. The first proposition may, perhaps, be conceded, the second scarcely. In any case, however, Mr. Edgeworth, who had a special leaning to the *jejune*, had a particular dislike to this form of fiction. "Why," he asked, "should the mind be filled with fantastic visions? Why should so much valuable time be lost? Why should we vitiate their taste and spoil their appetite by suffering them to feed upon sweetmeats?" Even poetical allusions, he thought, should be avoided in books for children. On the other hand, with the happy intuition he often displayed, he recognized that the current children's books of his time erred in introducing too much that was purely didactic, too many general reflections. He urged his daughter to avoid these errors, to bear action in view, and that whether in morals or in science, the thing to be taught should seem to arise from the circumstances in which the little persons of the drama were placed. He saw that in order to prevent precepts from tiring the eye and mind, it was necessary to make the stories in which they were introduced dramatic, to keep alive hope, fear and curiosity by some degree of intricacy.

Admirably did his daughter carry out the precepts he thus laid down. It was Miss Edgeworth who really inaugurated for England the reign of didactic fiction. Though never losing sight of her aim, she also never lost sight of the amusement of her young readers. She rightly comprehended that only by captivating their senses could she conquer and influence their reason. Her children's tales, written with motion and spirit, were told in the simple language of the young. She went straight to the hearts of her little readers because they could understand her; they needed no grown person to explain to them sesquipedalian words. There is a freshness about her stories that children are quick to respond to, and it arises from the fact that the children she depicts for her readers are real. Miss Edgeworth knew what children were like; she saw them not only from without but from within; she had lived all her life among little people. Their world never became a paradise from which she was shut out. The advantages she thus enjoyed were as rare as they are important for the due comprehension of the needs of childhood, and she utilized them to the utmost. The chief charm of her tales, that which makes them *sui generis* both now and then, is that she not only wrote in the language of children, but, what is even rarer, from the child's point of view.

There are yet among us those who owe their earliest pleasures to Miss Edgeworth, and if of late she has been somewhat jostled out of the nursery and school-room because it is the tendency of the modern child to revolt against all attempts to teach it unawares, we are far from sure that the change is wholly for the better. It was a just perception of this that caused Miss Yonge to say in *The Stokesley Secret* that her heroes "would read any books that made no pretensions to be instructive, but even a fact about a lion or an elephant made them detect wisdom in disguise, and throw it aside." The modern child finds, it is said, Miss Edgeworth's tales dry; American books of a semi-novelistic character, rattling stories of wild adventure, are preferred.

This may be so, but we cannot help thinking that, just in these days, when the ethical standard held up to children is not too high, a judicious admixture of these works with Miss Edgeworth's high-minded stories, inculcating self-sacrifice, unselfishness, obedience, and other neglected virtues, might be of great advantage. There are sundry of Miss Edgeworth's children's tales that are truly engrossing, veritable masterpieces of style and execution. Who is there, no matter how advanced his age, who cannot read with pleasure the tales of *Lazy Lawrence, Tarlton, The Bracelets, Waste Not Want Not, Forgive and Forget, e tutti quanti?* Who is there whom it much disturbs that the account of Eton Montem is not accurate, and that perhaps there could have been nothing more unfortunate than to lay the scene of action of *The Little Merchants* in Naples, the one spot in all the earth where the events therein described could not have happened? Change the name of the locality, the charm of the tale remains and the absurdity is removed. Nor must it be forgotten that children, less well read than their elders, are less alive to these blemishes, which are, after all, of no real import. Of *Simple Susan*, so great a person as Sir Walter Scott said that "when the boy brings back the lamb to the little girl, there is nothing for it but to put down the book and cry." Then as to *Rosamond*, who does not feel a true affection for that impetuous, impulsive little girl, and who is there (so greatly have our ideas of morality changed) that does not think that in the matter of the famous *Purple Jar*, an unjustifiable trick was played upon her by her mother? It was a part of the Edgeworth system to make misdirected or mistaken desires stultify themselves; but the child should have been informed of the nature of the jar, and if then she still persisted in her choice, she would have been fairly treated, which now she is not. *Frank* remains a capital book for little people, and if, occasionally, Miss Edgeworth's juvenile tales reflect too much of the stiff wisdom of her age, these are matters which children, not morally *blasé*, hardly remark. On the other hand, there is never anything mawkish in her pages, she never fills the mind with yearnings for the impossible, she never works too much upon the susceptibilities, which modern child-literature so often does. Her writings for children are certainly *sui generis*, not because she has attempted what has never been attempted before, but because she succeeded where others failed. She made even her youngest reader comprehend that virtue is its own reward, while avoiding the error invariably fallen into by writers for the young, of representing virtues as always triumphant, vice as uniformly punished—a fallacy even children are quick to detect. It has been objected to her that she checks enthusiasm, the source of some of the noblest actions of mankind. This is true; she has somewhat erred on the repressive side, but her purpose was right and good. She saw plainly that enthusiasm, generous in its origin, is but too often the source of misfortune, ill-judged effort, and consequent disappointment. Moderation, the duties of contentment and industry, are what she loves to uphold; the lower, humbler, but no less effective virtues of existence.

On the other hand it is clear, from her letters, that she herself was not devoid of enthusiasm, and here, again, it was probably her father's influence that made her exclude it from her writings. In one of her letters she says:—

Vive l'enthousiasme! Without it characters may be very snug and comfortable in the world, but there is a degree of happiness which they will never taste, and of which they have no more idea than an oyster can have.

Harry and Lucy falls sharply into two parts. The earlier portion was intended to be read before *Rosamond*, and after *Frank*; the latter was the last of the juvenile series. The work had been begun by Mr. Edgeworth and his wife Honora, from the need of a book to follow Mrs. Barbauld's lessons, and as a story to be inserted in this work Mr. Day had originally written *Sandford and Merton*. *Harry and Lucy* was printed, but not published. It was kept, as originally meant, only for the Edgeworth children; but after more than twenty years Mr. Edgeworth passed the work on to his daughter, and bade her complete it and prepare it for publication. The first portion thus came out early in the century, while the last part did not appear till 1825.

Harry and Lucy is unquestionably heavy in parts, especially the latter half, yet first principles are well explained and popularized, and instruction and tale so skillfully blended that the young reader cannot skip the one and read the other. The main idea and the chief merit of these volumes, not at once perhaps obvious, is that of enforcing in a popular form the necessity of exercising the faculties of children, so that they should be, in part, their own instructors, and of adding to those more common incentives to study, which consist of rewards and punishments, the far surer, nobler and more effective stimulus of curiosity kept alive by variety and the pleasure of successful invention. It was the desire of the authors to show with what ease the faculty of thinking may be cultivated in children, a point on which Miss Edgeworth insists in other of her tales. In *Harry and Lucy* are explained simply and familiarly, sometimes in conversations between the children and their parents and friends, sometimes in dialogue between the children themselves, the rudiments of science, principally of chemistry and physics, and the application of these to the common purposes of life. And herein we again encounter one of the grand merits of the Edgeworths, which we can to-day better appreciate than their contemporaries. They saw clearly what in their day was apprehended only by very few, the importance that the study of science was to acquire in the future. Miss Edgeworth says:—

My father long ago foresaw that the taste for scientific as well as literary knowledge, which has risen so rapidly and spread so widely, would render it necessary to make some provision for the early instruction of youth in science, in addition to the great and successful attention paid to classical literatures.

And even apart from the immense importance of science in our daily life, science is, of all studies, that best suited to the growth of a child's mental powers. Novelty and variety are the spells of early life, and to work these well and helpfully is the greatest good that can be done to young people. Miss Edgeworth, in *Harry and Lucy*, as a whole succeeds in rousing her reader's curiosity without making them suspect design, and avoids all idea of a task. Thus the leading principles of science are unfolded in familiar experiments which give young learners the delight they would have in playing some interesting game, exercising their ingenuity without tiring them. Then, having once felt the pleasures of success, a permanent incentive to knowledge is induced, which it remains with the parents or tutors to improve. The books are obviously not such as are meant to be read at a sitting, and therefore can only be put into the hands of young people with judicious care. But in the Edgeworths' time neither old nor young devoured books after the manner of to-day. The apparently desultory and accidental plan of the book was really designed, purpose and moral being more skillfully disguised than is the case with Miss Edgeworth's tales for her equals. One of its great charms lies in the characters of the principal *dramatis personæ*, whose temperaments are exquisitely sketched, maintained and contrasted. Lucy, the lively, playful girl, who often allows her imagination to go rambling far afield from her judgment, a little inclined to be volatile, loving a joke, is cousin german to Rosamond, and, like this little girl, truly lovable. She supplies the lighter element, while the sterner is supplied by Harry, the brother she idolizes, who is partly her companion, partly her teacher. He has a sure and steady rather than a brilliant and rapid intellect, great mental curiosity and great patience in acquiring information. He is more apt to discern differences than to perceive resemblances, and therefore he does not always understand the wit and fun of Lucy, which at times even provoke him. In the conversations between them there is much judicious sprinkling of childish banter and nonsense, "an alloy necessary to make sense work well," to use Miss Edgeworth's own expressive words. A pity that the ever-delightful "Great Panjandrum" therein introduced is not her own, but only a quotation from a little-known nonsense genius.

This sequel to *Harry and Lucy* was far from finding universal favor. Sir Walter Scott wrote of it to Joanna Baillie:—

I have not the pen of our friend Miss Edgeworth, who writes all the while she laughs, talks, eats and drinks, and I believe, though I do not pretend to be so far in the secret, all the time she sleeps too. She has good luck in having a pen which walks at once so unweariedly and so well. I do not, however, quite like her last book on education (*Harry and Lucy*), considered as a general work. She should have limited the title to *Education in Natural Philosophy*, or some such term, for there is no great use in teaching children in general to roof houses or build bridges, which, after all, a carpenter or a mason does a great deal better at 2s. 6d. a day. Your ordinary Harry should be kept to his grammar, and your Lucy of most common occurrence would be kept employed on her sampler, instead of wasting wood and cutting their fingers, which I am convinced they did, though their historian says nothing of it.

That both she and her father exacted much from their pupils and readers is beyond question, but they regarded this as a wholesome effort, and they were probably right. One thing is certain: that whatever their shortcomings, Miss Edgeworth's children's tales exercised a wide, deep and lasting influence over a long range of time, and nothing of equal or even approximate importance arose coeval with them. It was she who first brought rational morality to the level of the comprehension of childhood, who taught the language of virtue and truth in the alphabet of the young, thus forestalling the teaching of schools by her rare power of combining ethics with entertainment. Miss Edgeworth can still with advantage and pleasure hold her own even upon the present well-stocked nursery book-shelves, and it might be well for the next generation if we saw her there a little oftener. Better Miss Edgeworth any day, with all her arid utilitarianism, her realism, than the sickly sentimental unrealities of a far too popular modern school.

CHAPTER VI.

IRISH AND MORAL TALES.

IN 1800 was published anonymously a small book called *Castle Rackrent*. It professed to be a Hibernian tale, taken from facts and from the manners of the Irish squires before the year 1782. It proved to be a most entertaining, witty history of the fortunes of an Irish estate, told professedly by an illiterate, partial old steward, who recounted the story of the Rackrent family in his vernacular with the full confidence that the affairs of Sir Patrick, Sir Murtagh, Sir Kit and Sir Condy were as interesting to all the world as they were to himself. *Honest* Thaby, as this curious but characteristic specimen of Irish good humor, fidelity and wrong-headedness was pleased to call himself, having no conception of the true application of this epithet, had certainly shown literary perception, or rather his creator for him. For this was no other than Maria Edgeworth, who stood confessed upon the title-page of the second edition that was clamorously demanded within a few months of issue. The confession was wrung from her because some one had not only asserted that he was the author, but had actually taken the trouble to copy out several pages with corrections and erasures, as if it were his original manuscript. It was in this work that Miss Edgeworth first struck her own peculiar vein, and had she never written anything but *Castle Rackrent* her fame could not have died. It is a page torn from the national history of Ireland, inimitable, perennially delightful, equally humorous and pathetic, holding up with shrewd wit and keen perception, mingled with sympathetic indulgence, the follies and vices that have caused, and in a modified degree still cause, no small proportion of the social miseries that have afflicted and still afflict that unhappy land.

Here are portrayed a series of Irish landlords with their odd discrepancies and striking individualities, alternately drunken, litigious, pugilistic, slovenly and densely ignorant; or else easy, extravagant and good-natured to the point of vice; all, however, of one mind in being profoundly indifferent to their own or their tenants' welfare. The sharp contrasts of the magnificent and paltry that characterized their state of living, with the mixed confidence in a special Providence and their own good luck that distinguished their muddle-headed mode of thought, is forcibly held up to view. No conclusions are drawn; the narrative, which never flags or drags, is rattled off with spirit, the abundant anecdotes are poured forth with true Irish exuberance, while the humor of the story arises in great measure from the sublime unconsciousness of the story-teller to the wit, naïvete or absurdity of his remarks. We are held spell-bound, we laugh and weep in a breath, we are almost over-persuaded by loyal old Thady to pardon the errors of the family, "one of the most ancient in the kingdom, related to the kings of Ireland, but that was before my time."

If there was an ulterior end in view in this story beyond that of recording national characteristics which she had had peculiarly good opportunities for observing, and which she here reproduced from the life with broad, full strokes, Miss Edgeworth has masked it so happily that it does not obtrude itself. The society and manners of the Irish are painted as equally provoking and endearing. The book is an epitome of the Irish character, "fighting like devils for conciliation, and hating one another for the love of God." Never did laughter and tears, sympathy and repugnance, lie more closely together than in this tale. It is curious to read the author's prefatory apology when there are still alive, in every exasperated form, the very conditions she thinks belong to a state of things rapidly passing away, "owing to the probable loss of Irish identity after the union with England." The supposed "obsolete prejudices and animosities of race" are unhappily still extant. Perhaps it is partly this fact that makes Miss Edgeworth's Irish tales so fresh to this day. But only in part; on their own account alone they are delightful, and *Castle Rackrent* even more than the rest.

We have Mrs. Barbauld's testimony that Miss Edgeworth wrote *Castle Rackrent* unassisted by her father, and judging how infinitely superior in spontaneity, flexibility, and nervousness of style, force, pith and boldness, it is to those of her writings with which he meddled, it is forcibly impressed upon us that Mr. Edgeworth's literary tinkering of his daughter's works was far from being to their advantage. Her next published book was her first attempt to deal with the novel proper. In *Belinda* she strove to delineate the follies and hollowness of fashionable life. The heroine is rather a lifeless puppet; but the more truly prominent figure, Lady Delacour, is drawn with power and keen intuition. A woman of gay and frivolous antecedents, striving to rise into a higher atmosphere under the ennobling influences of a pure friendship, and finding the task a difficult one, was no easy character to draw or to sustain. Had Lady Delacour died heroically, as Miss Edgeworth had planned, and as the whole course of the story leads the reader to expect, the book would have been a success. But to allow her to recover, to cause her to evolve a reformed character after a type psychologically impossible to one of her temperament, weakened the force of the foregoing pages and rendered them untrue. Again, it is on Miss Edgeworth's spoken testimony to Mrs. Barbauld that we learn that she meant to make Lady Delacour die, but that it was her father who suggested the alteration; and since it was a part of the Edgeworthian creed to believe in such simple and sudden reformations, she accepted his counsel, to the artistic injury of her tale. It was Mr. Edgeworth, too, who wrote and interpolated the worthless and high-flown Virginia episode, in which Clarence Harvey takes to the freak of wife-training after the pattern of Mr. Day. This incident is quite out of keeping with the character of Clarence, who is depicted a wooden dandy, but not a romantic fool. These changes, willingly submitted to by Miss Edgeworth, who had the most unbounded belief in her father's superior wisdom on all points whatsoever, also mark his idiosyncracy, for Mr. Edgeworth was a most rare and curious compound of utilitarianism and wild romance.

It is almost possible, in Miss Edgeworth's works, to venture to point out the passages that have been tampered with and those where she has been allowed free play. Thus there are portions of *Belinda* in which she is as much at her best as in *Castle Rackrent*, or other of her masterpieces. Who but she could have penned the lively description given by Sir Philip Baddeley of the fêtes at Frogmore? How exquisitely is this ill-natured fool made to paint himself, how truthful is the picture, free from any taint of exaggeration! Sir Philip's endeavor to disgust Belinda with Clarence Harvey, his manner of attempting it, and his final proposal, is a very masterpiece of caustic humor.

Belinda was no favorite with Miss Edgeworth. Writing to Mrs. Barbauld some years later, she says:—

Belinda is but an uninteresting personage after all.... I was not either in *Belinda* or *Leonora* sufficiently aware that the *goodness* of a heroine interests only in proportion to the perils and trials to which it is exposed.

And again, after revising it for republication, she says:—

I really was so provoked with the cold tameness of that stick or stone, Belinda, that I could have torn the pages to pieces; really I have not the heart or the patience to *correct* her. As the hackney coachman said, "Mend *you*! Better make a new one."

Miss Edgeworth was therefore capable of self-criticism. Indeed, at no time did she set even a due value on her own work, still less an exaggerated one. To the day of her death she sincerely believed that all the honor and glory she had reaped belonged of right to her father alone. But there was yet another reason why Miss Edgeworth never liked *Belinda*. She was staying at Black Castle when the first printed copy reached her. Before her aunt saw it she contrived to tear out the title-pages of the three volumes, and Mrs. Ruxton thus read it without the least suspicion as to its authorship. She was much delighted, and insisted on reading out to her niece passage after passage. Miss Edgeworth pretended to be deeply interested in some book she was herself reading, and when Mrs. Ruxton exclaimed, "Is not that admirably written?" replied, "Admirably read, I think." "It may not be so very good," added Mrs. Ruxton, "but it shows just the sort of knowledge of high life which people have who live in the world." But in vain she appealed to Miss Edgeworth for sympathy, until, provoked by her faint acquiescence,

Mrs. Ruxton at last accused her of being envious. "I am sorry to see my little Maria unable to bear the praises of a rival author." This remark made Miss Edgeworth burst into tears and show her aunt the title-pages of the book. But Mrs. Ruxton was not pleased; she never wholly liked *Belinda* afterwards, and Miss Edgeworth had always a painful recollection that her aunt had suspected her of the meanness of envy.

In 1802 was published the *Essay on Irish Bulls*, bearing on its title-page the names of father and daughter. Its title appears to have misled even the Irish: at least it is related that an Irish gentleman, secretary to an agricultural society, who was much interested in improving the breed of Irish cattle, sent for it, expecting to find a work on live stock. We have Miss Edgeworth's own account of the genesis of the book:—

The first design of the essay was my father's: under the semblance of attack, he wished to show the English public the eloquence, wit and talents of the lower classes of people in Ireland. Working zealously upon the ideas which he suggested, sometimes what was spoken by him was afterwards written by me; or when I wrote my first thoughts, they were corrected and improved by him; so that no book was ever written more completely in partnership. On this, as on most subjects, whether light or serious, when we wrote together, it would now be difficult, almost impossible, to recollect which thoughts originally were his and which were mine. All passages in which there are Latin quotations or classical allusions must be his exclusively, because I am entirely ignorant of the learned languages. The notes on the Dublin shoe-black's metaphorical language I recollect are chiefly his.

I have heard him tell that story with all the natural, indescribable Irish tones and gestures, of which written language can give but a faint idea. He excelled in imitating the Irish, because he never overstepped the modesty or the assurance of nature. He marked exquisitely the happy confidence, the shrewd wit of the people, without condescending to produce effect by caricature. He knew not only their comic talents, but their powers of pathos; and often when he had just heard from them some pathetic complaint, he has repeated it to me while the impression was fresh. In the chapter on wit and eloquence in *Irish Bulls* there is a speech of a poor freeholder to a candidate who asked for his vote; this speech was made to my father when he was canvassing the county of Longford. It was repeated to me a few hours afterwards, and I wrote it down instantly, without, I believe, the variation of a word.

The complaint of a poor widow against her landlord, and his reply, were quoted by Campbell in his *Lectures on Eloquence*, as happy specimens, under the conviction that they were fictitious. Miss Edgeworth assures us that they are "unembellished facts," that her father was the magistrate before whom the complaint and defense were made, and that she wrote down the speeches word for word as he repeated them to her. This *Essay on Irish Bulls*, though a somewhat rambling and discursive composition, is a readable one, full of good stories, pathetic and humorous. Besides giving critical and apt illustrations, the authors did justice to the better traits of the Irish character. It was an earnest vindication of the national intellect from the charge of habitual blundering, showing how blundering is common to all countries, and is no more Irish than Persian. They further proved that most so-called bulls are no bulls at all, but often a poetic license, a heart-spoken effusion, and that thus the offense became a grace beyond the reach of art.

Moral Tales also saw the light in 1801. They too were written to illustrate *Practical Education*, but aimed at readers of a more advanced age than the children's tales; in fact, both here and elsewhere Miss Edgeworth strove to do on a larger scale what was achieved by the ancient form of parable, to make an attractive medium for the instruction and conviction of minds. It was a fancy of hers, and perhaps a characteristic of her age, when female authorship was held in somewhat doubtful repute, that she invariably insisted on appearing before the public under cover of her father's name. He therefore wrote for *Moral Tales*, as afterwards for all her works, one of his ludicrously bombastic prefaces, which, whatever they may have done in his own time, would certainly to-day be the most effective means of repelling readers. The stories are six in number: *Forester, The Prussian Vase, The Good Aunt, Angelina, The Good French Governess,* and *Mademoiselle Panache.* Of these the plots are for the most part poorly contrived, the narrative hammered out *invita Minerva,* and, owing to their aim, nothing capricious or accidental is permitted. Too obviously they are the mature fruits of purpose and reflection, not happy effusions of the fancy, and hence also not always successful. Sometimes the fault lay with the subject that afforded too little scope, sometimes the moral striven after did not admit of the embellishments requisite for a work of amusement. One thing, however, is certain: that Miss Edgeworth honestly endeavored to combine entertainment with instruction, and that, taken as a whole, she succeeded. She did not shelter herself behind the saying that *Il est permis d'ennuyer en moralités d'ici jusqu'à Constantinople.* But it is the key to her writings, to their excellences and their defects, that the duty of a moral teacher was always uppermost in her mind. Her aim was not to display her own talents, but to make her readers substantially better and happier, to show how easy and agreeable to practice are high principles. Again and again she insists, with irrefragable force, that it is the ordinary and attainable qualities of life rather than the lofty and heroic ones on which our substantial happiness depends, an insistance new in the domain of fiction, which as a rule preaches other doctrines. With this end in view she had necessarily to sacrifice some freedom and grace of invention to illustrate her moral aphorisms, her salutary truths, and she yielded to the temptation to exaggerate in order to make her work more impressive. Her *Moral Tales* are a series of climaces of instances, an enlargement of La Bruyère's idea, a method allowable to creations of fancy, but not quite justifiable when applied to the probable. Moreover, it was a feature of the eighteenth century, to which in many respects Miss Edgeworth belonged, that its tales and novels were not analytic. Psychology based upon biology was as yet unknown, or in so empirical a stage as to be remote from practical application. The writers of those days depict their characters not as the complex bundles of good and bad qualities and potentialities that even the veriest scribbler paints them to-day, but as sharply good or bad, so that one flaw of character, one vice, one folly, was made to be the origin of all their disasters. It is, of course, always dangerous when the author plays the part of Providence, and can twist the narrative to suit the moral; but this censure applies to all moral tales, by no matter whom. Miss Edgeworth strove to civilize and instruct by the rehearsal of a tale, and if we all, from the perversity of human nature, rather revolt against being talked to for our good, it must ever be added in her praise that she generally allures us and makes us listen to her maxims of right living. Her self-imposed task was neither humble nor easy, but one that required judgment, patience and much knowledge of the world; her moral wholesomeness cannot be rated too highly or be too much commended. If she ascribed too large a share of morality to the head instead of the heart, this was the result of the doctrines with which her father had imbued her.

The most successful of the *Moral Tales* is beyond question *Angelina*. Its moral is not obtrusive, its fable is well constructed, the tale is told with point, spirit, gentle but incisive satire. The sentimental young lady, a female Don Quixote, roaming the world in search of an unknown friend whose acquaintance she has made solely through the medium of her writings, is a genus that is not extinct. Never has Miss Edgeworth been happier than here, when she combats her heroine's errors, not by serious arguments, but with the shafts of ridicule. The tale is a gem. *Forester*, on the other hand, for which Mr. Edgeworth claims that it is a male version of the same character, does not strike us in that light, nor is it as perfect in conception or execution. The character of the eccentric youth who scorns the common forms of civilized society, and is filled with visionary schemes of benevolence and happiness, was based, it would seem, upon that of Mr. Day, and, as a portrait, was doubtless a happy one. But the hero fails to interest, his aberrations are simply foolish, the means whereby he is redeemed too mechanical and crude, the whole both too detailed and too much condensed to hold our attention or to seem probable. *The Good French Governess* embodies the Edgeworthian mode of giving lessons, which was to make them pleasures, not tasks, to the pupils; maxims now universally recognized and practiced, but new in the days when for little children there were no pleasant roads to learning in the shape of *kindergärten*. *The Good Aunt* insists upon the necessity of home example and instruction, the lack of which no school training can supply. It is the weakest of all the tales, and verges dangerously upon the namby-pamby. *Mademoiselle Panache*, according to Mr. Edgeworth, is "a sketch of the necessary consequences of imprudently trusting the happiness of a daughter to the care of those who can teach nothing but accomplishments;" but which, according to most readers, will be pronounced the melancholy result of an ignorance that could mistake an illiterate French milliner for an accomplished French governess. It is unjust to lay the results of the tuition of such a personage to the charge of that favorite scape-goat—the frivolity of the French nation. *The Prussian Vase*, a tale, again according to Mr. Edgeworth, "designed principally for young gentlemen who are intended for the bar," is a pretty but apocryphal anecdote attributed to Frederic the Great, of a nature impossible to the mental bias of that enlightened despot. It is, moreover, an eulogium of the English mode of trial by jury.

Taken as a whole, these tales may be said to enforce the doctrine that unhappiness is more often the result of defects of character than of external circumstances. Like all Miss Edgeworth's writings, they found instant favor and were translated into French and German. With no desire to detract from their merits, we cannot avoid the inference that this circumstance points to a great lack of contemporary foreign fiction of a pure and attractive kind.

CHAPTER VII.

IN FRANCE AND AT HOME.

THE peace, or rather the truce, of Amiens had induced many travellers to visit France. They all returned enraptured with what they had seen of society in Paris, and with the masterpieces of art dragged thither, as the spoils of military despotism. Letters from some of these tourists awakened in Mr. Edgeworth a wish to revisit France. The desire took shape as resolve after the visit to Edgeworthstown of M. Pictet, of Geneva, who promised the family letters of introduction to, and a cordial welcome among, the thinkers of the land. As translator of *Practical Education*, and as the editor of the *Bibliothèque Britannique*,[5] in which he had published most of Miss Edgeworth's *Moral Tales*, and detailed criticisms of both father and daughter, he had certainly prepared the way for their favorable reception. The tour was therefore arranged for the autumn of 1802, a roomy coach was purchased, and in September Mr., Mrs., Miss and Miss Charlotte Edgeworth started for their continental trip.

The series of letters Miss Edgeworth wrote home during this time are most entertaining, unaffected, sprightly and graphic. She often sketches a character, a national peculiarity, with a touch, while on the other hand she does not shirk detail if only she can succeed in presenting a vivid picture of all she is beholding to those dear ones at home who are debarred from the same enjoyment. Carnarvon, Bangor, Etruria and Leicester were visited on the way out. At Leicester Miss Edgeworth had an amusing adventure:—

Handsome town, good shops. Walked, whilst dinner was getting ready, to a circulating library. My father asked for *Belinda*, *Bulls*, etc.: found they were in good repute; *Castle Rackrent* in better—the others often borrowed, but *Castle Rackrent* often bought. The bookseller, an open-hearted man, begged us to look at a book of poems just published by a Leicester lady, a Miss Watts. I recollected to have seen some years ago a specimen of this lady's proposed translation of Tasso, which my father had highly admired. He told the bookseller that we would pay our respects to Miss Watts if it would be agreeable to her. When we had dined we set out with our enthusiastic bookseller. We were shown by the light of a lantern along a very narrow passage between high walls, to the door of a decent-looking house: a maid-servant, candle in hand, received us. "Be pleased, ladies, to walk up stairs." A neatish room, nothing extraordinary in it except the inhabitants: Mrs. Watts, a tall, black-eyed, prim, dragon-looking woman, in the background; Miss Watts, a tall young lady in white, fresh color, fair, thin, oval face, rather pretty. The moment Mrs. Edgeworth entered, Miss Watts, taking her for the authoress, darted forward with arms, long thin arms, outstretched to their, utmost swing. "Oh, what an honor this is!" each word and syllable rising in tone till the last reached a scream. Instead of embracing my mother, as her first action threatened, she started back to the farthest end of the room, which was not light enough to show her attitude distinctly, but it seemed to be intended to express the receding of awestruck admiration—stopped by the wall. Charlotte and I passed by unnoticed, and seated ourselves, by the old lady's desire; she, after many twistings of her wrists, elbows and neck, all of which appeared to be dislocated, fixed herself in her arm-chair, resting her hands on the black mahogany splayed elbows. Her person was no sooner at rest than her eyes and all her features began to move in all directions. She looked like a nervous and suspicious person electrified. She seemed to be the acting partner in this house, to watch over her treasure of a daughter, to supply her with wordly wisdom, to look upon her as a phœnix, and—scold her.

Miss Watts was all ecstasy and lifting up of hands and eyes, speaking always in that loud, shrill, theatrical tone with which a puppet-master supplies his puppets. I all the time sat like a mouse. My father asked, "Which of those ladies, madam, do you think is your sister-authoress?" "I am no physiognomist"—in a screech—"but I do imagine that to be the lady," bowing, as she sat, almost to the ground, and pointing to Mrs. Edgeworth. "No; guess again." "Then that must be she," bowing to Charlotte. "No." "Then this lady," looking forward to see what sort of an animal I was, for she had never seen me till this instant. To make me some amends, she now drew her chair close to me and began to pour forth praises: "Lady Delacour, oh! *Letters for Literary Ladies*, oh!"

Now for the pathetic part. This poor girl sold a novel in four volumes for ten guineas to Lane. My father is afraid, though she has considerable talents, to recommend her to Johnson, lest she should not answer! Poor girl! what a pity she had no friend to direct her talents! How much she made me feel the value of mine!

After a trip through the Low Countries, the travellers entered France and received many civilities in all the towns they passed through, thanks to the fact that the *Bibliothéque Britannique* was taken in every public library. At Paris the Edgeworths were admitted into the best society of the period, which consisted of the remains of the French nobility, and of men of letters and science. The old Abbé Morellet, "respected as one of the most *reasonable* of all the wits of France," the *doyen* of French literature, was a previous acquaintance. By his introductions and those of M. Pictet, added to the prestige of their own names and their relationship to the Abbé Edgeworth, the most exclusive houses were opened to the family, and they thus became acquainted with every one worth knowing, among whom were La Harpe,

Madame de Genlis, Kosciusko, Madame Récamier, the Comte de Ségur, Dumont, Suard, Camille Jordan. In all circles the subject of politics was carefully avoided; the company held themselves aloof, and wilfully ignored the important issues that were surging around them; their conversation turned chiefly on new plays, novels and critical essays. As is usual in such small circles with limited interests, a good deal of mutual admiration was practiced, and the Edgeworths received their due share.

At the Abbé Morellet's Miss Edgeworth met Madame d'Oudinot, Rousseau's "Julie." This is her impression:—

Julie is now seventy-two years of age, a thin woman in a little black bonnet; she appeared to me shockingly ugly; she squints so much that it is impossible to tell which way she is looking; but no sooner did I hear her speak than I began to like her, and no sooner was I seated beside her than I began to find in her countenance a most benevolent and agreeable expression. She entered into conversation immediately; her manner invited and could not fail to obtain confidence. She seems as gay and open-hearted as a girl of fifteen. It has been said of her that she not only never did any harm, but never suspected any. She is possessed of that art which Lord Kaimes said he would prefer to the finest gift from the queen of the fairies: the art of seizing the best side of every object. She has had great misfortunes, but she has still retained the power of making herself and her friends happy. Even during the horrors of the Revolution, if she met with a flower, a butterfly, an agreeable smell, a pretty color, she would turn her attention to these, and for a moment suspend the sense of misery—not from frivolity, but from real philosophy. No one has exerted themselves with more energy in the service of her friends. I felt in her company the delightful influence of a cheerful temper and soft, attractive manners—enthusiasm which age cannot extinguish, and which spends, but does not waste itself on small but not trifling objects. I wish I could at seventy-two be such a woman! She told me that Rousseau, whilst he was writing so finely on education, and leaving his own children in the Foundling Hospital, defended himself with so much eloquence that even those who blamed him in their hearts could not find tongues to answer him. Once at dinner at Madame d'Oudinot's there was a fine pyramid of fruit. Rousseau in helping himself took the peach which formed the base of the pyramid, and the rest fell immediately. "Rousseau," said she, "that is what you always do with all our systems; you pull down with a single touch; but who will build up what you pull down?" I asked if he was grateful for all the kindness shown to him. "No, he was ungrateful; he had a thousand bad qualities, but I turned my attention from them to his genius and the good he had done mankind."

La Harpe was visited in his own home:—

He lives in a wretched house, and we went up dirty stairs, through dirty passages, where I wondered how fine ladies' trains and noses could go; and were received in a dark, small den by the philosopher, or rather *dévot*, for he spurns the name of philosopher. He was in a dirty, reddish night-gown, and very dirty night-cap bound round the forehead with a superlatively dirty, chocolate-colored ribbon. Madame Récamier, the beautiful, the elegant, robed in white satin, trimmed with white fur, seated herself on the elbow of his arm-chair, and besought him to repeat his verses. Charlotte has drawn a picture of this scene.

An interesting visit was also paid to Madame de Genlis:—

She had previously written to say she would be glad to be personally acquainted with Mr. and Miss Edgeworth. She lives—where do you think?— where Sully used to live, at the Arsenal. Bonaparte has given her apartments there. Now, I do not know what you imagine in reading Sully's memoirs, but I always imagined that the Arsenal was one large building with a façade to it, like a very large hotel or a palace, and I fancied it was somewhere in the middle of Paris. On the contrary, it is quite in the suburbs. We drove on and on, and at last we came to a heavy archway, like what you see at the entrance to a fortified town. We drove under it for the length of three or four yards in total darkness, and then we found ourselves, as well as we could see by the light of some dim lamps, in a large square court surrounded by buildings: here we thought we were to alight. No such thing: the coachman drove under another thick archway, lighted at the entrance by a single lamp. We found ourselves in another court, and still we went on, archway after archway, court after court, in all which reigned desolate silence. I thought the archways and the courts and the desolate silence would never end. At last the coachman stopped, and asked for the tenth time where the lady lived. It is excessively difficult to find people in Paris; we thought the names of Madame de Genlis and the Arsenal would have been sufficient; but the whole of this congregation of courts and gateways and houses is called the Arsenal; and hundreds and hundreds of people inhabit it who are probably perfect strangers to Madame de Genlis. At the doors where our coachman inquired, some answered that they knew nothing of her; some that she lived in the Faubourg St. Germain; others believed that she might be at Passy; others had heard that she had apartments given to her by the Government somewhere in the Arsenal, but could not tell where. While the coachman thus begged his way, we, anxiously looking out at him from the middle of the great square where we were left, listened for the answers that were given, and which often from the distance escaped our ears. At last a door pretty near to us opened, and our coachman's head and hat were illuminated by the candle held by the person who opened the door; and as the two figures parted from each other, we could distinctly see the expression of the countenances and their lips move. The result of this parley was successful; we were directed to the house where Madame de Genlis lived, and thought all difficulties ended. No such thing; her apartments were still to be sought for. We saw before us a large, crooked, ruinous stone staircase, lighted by a single bit of candle hanging in a vile tin lantern, in an angle of the bare wall at the turn of the staircase— only just light enough to see that the walls were bare and old, and the stairs immoderately dirty. There were no signs of the place being inhabited except this lamp, which could not have been lighted without hands. I stood still in melancholy astonishment, while my father groped his way into a kind of porter's lodge or den at the foot of the stairs, where he found a man who was porter to various people who inhabited this house. You know the Parisian houses are inhabited by hordes of different people, and the stairs are in fact streets, and dirty streets, to their dwellings. The porter, who was neither obliging nor intelligent, carelessly said that "*Madame de Genlis logeait au seconde à gauche, qu'il faudrait tirer sa sonnette*"—he believed she was at home if she was not gone out. Up we went by ourselves, for this porter, though we were strangers and pleaded that we were so, never offered to stir a step to guide or to light us. When we got to the second stage, we finally saw, by the light from the one candle at the first landing-place, two dirty, large folding doors, one set on the right and one on the left, and having on each a bell no larger than what you see in the small parlor of a small English inn. My father pulled one bell and waited some minutes—no answer; pulled the other bell and waited—no answer; thumped at the left door—no answer; pushed and pulled at it—could not open it; pushed open one of the right-hand folding doors— utter darkness; went in as well as we could feel—there was no furniture. After we had been there a few seconds we could discern the bare walls and some strange lumber in one corner. The room was a prodigious height, like an old play-house, and we went down again to the stupid or surly porter. He came up stairs very unwillingly, and pointed to a deep recess between the stairs and the folding doors: "*Allez! voilà la porte; tirez la sonnette.*" He and his candle went down, and my father had just time to seize the handle of the bell, when we were again in darkness. After ringing this feeble bell, we presently heard doors open and little footsteps approaching nigh. The door was opened by a girl of about Honora's size, holding an ill-set-up, wavering candle in her hand, the light of which fell full upon her face and figure. Her face was remarkably intelligent, dark, sparkling eyes, dark hair, curled in the most fashionable long corkscrew ringlets over her eyes and cheeks. She parted the ringlets to take a full view of us, and we were equally impatient to take a full view of her. The dress of her figure by no means suited the head and the elegance of her attitude. What her "nether weeds" might be we could not distinctly see, but they seemed to be a coarse, short petticoat, like what Molly Bristow's children would wear, not on Sundays; a woolen gray spencer above, pinned with a single pin by the lapels tight across the neck under the chin, and open all below. After surveying us and hearing that our name was Edgeworth, she smiled graciously and bid us follow her, saying, "*Maman est chez elle.*" She led the way with the grace of a young lady who has been taught to dance, across two ante-chambers, miserable-looking, but miserable or not, no house in Paris can be without them. The girl or young lady, for we were still in doubt which to think her, led us into a small room, in which the candles were so well screened by a green tin screen that we could scarcely distinguish the tall form of a lady in black who rose from her arm-chair by the fireside as the door opened; a great puff of smoke came from the huge fireplace at the same moment. She came forward, and we made our way towards her as well as we could through a confusion of tables, chairs and work-baskets, china, writing-desks and inkstands, and bird-cages and a harp. She did not speak, and as her back was now turned to both fire and candle I could not see her face, nor anything but the outline of her form and her attitude. Her form was the remains of a fine form, and her attitude that of a woman used to a better drawing-room. I, being foremost, and she silent, was compelled to speak to the figure in darkness: "*Madame de Genlis nous a fait l'honneur de nous mander qu'elle voulait bien nous permettre de lui rendre visite, et de lui offrir nos respects,*" said I, or words to that effect; to which she replied by taking my hand, and saying something in which "*charmée*" was the most intelligible word. Whilst she spoke she looked over my shoulder at my father, whose bow, I presume, told her he was a gentleman, for she spoke to him immediately as if she wished to please, and seated us in fauteuils near the fire. I then had a full view of her face and figure. She looked like the full-length picture of my great-grandmother Edgeworth you may have seen in the garret, very thin and melancholy, but her face not so handsome as my grandmother's; dark eyes, long sallow cheeks, compressed thin lips, two or three black ringlets on a high forehead, a cap that Mrs. Grier might wear—altogether an appearance of fallen fortunes, worn-out health, and excessive but guarded irritability. To me there was nothing of that engaging, captivating manner which I had been taught to expect by many even of her enemies. She seemed to me to be alive only to literary quarrels and jealousies; the muscles of her face as she spoke, or my father spoke to her, quickly and too easily expressed hatred and anger whenever any not of her own party were mentioned. She is now, you know, *dévote acharnée.* When I mentioned with some enthusiasm the good Abbé Morellet, who has written so courageously in favor of the French exiled nobility and their children, she answered in a sharp voice: "*Oui, c'est un homme de beaucoup d'esprit, à ce qu'on je crois même, mais il faut apprendre qu'il n'est pas des Nôtres.*" My father spoke of Pamela, Lady Edward Fitzgerald, and explained how he had defended her in the Irish House of Commons. Instead of being pleased and touched, her mind instantly diverged into an elaborate and artificial exculpation of Lady Edward and herself, proving, or attempting to prove, that she never knew any of her husband's plans; that she utterly disapproved of them, at least of all she suspected of them.

This defense was quite lost upon us, who never thought of attacking; but Madame de Genlis seems to have been so much used to be attacked that she has defenses and apologies ready prepared, suited to all possible occasions. She spoke of Madame de Staël's *Delphine* with detestation; of another new and fashionable novel, *Amélie*, with abhorrence, and kissed my forehead twice because I had not read it; "*Vous autres Anglaises, vous êtes modestes!*" Where was Madame de Genlis' sense of delicacy when she penned and published *Les Chevaliers du Cigne?* Forgive, my dear Aunt Mary. You begged me to see her with favorable eyes, and I went to see her after seeing her *Rosière de Salency*, with the most favorable disposition, but I could not like her. There was something of malignity in her countenance and conversation that repelled love, and of hypocrisy which annihilated esteem; and from time to time I saw, or thought I saw, through the gloom of her countenance, a gleam of coquetry.[6] But my father judges much more favorably of her than I do. She evidently took pains to please him, and he says he is sure she is a person over whose mind he could gain great ascendancy. He thinks her a woman of violent passions, unbridled imagination and ill-tempered, but not malevolent; one who has been so torn to pieces that she now turns upon her enemies, and longs to tear in her turn. He says she has certainly great powers of pleasing, though I certainly neither saw nor felt them. But you know, my dear aunt, that I am not famous for judging sanely of strangers on a first visit, and I might be prejudiced or mortified by Madame de Genlis assuring me that she had never read anything of mine except *Belinda*, had heard of *Practical Education*, and heard it much praised, but had never seen it. She has just published an additional volume of her *Petits Romans*, in which there are some beautiful stories; but you must not expect another *Mademoiselle de Clermont*— one such story in an age is as much as one can reasonably expect.

I had almost forgotten to tell you that the little girl who showed us in is a girl whom she is educating. "*Elle m'appelle Maman, mais elle n'est pas ma fille.*" The manner in which this little girl spoke to Madame de Genlis, and looked at her, appeared to me more in her favor than anything else. She certainly spoke to her with freedom and fondness, and without any affectation. I went to look at what the child was writing. She was translating Darwin's *Zoonomia*. I read some of the translation; it was excellent. She was, I think she said, ten years old. It is certain that Madame de Genlis made the present Duke of Orleans[7] such an excellent mathematician, that when he was, during his emigration, in distress for bread, he taught mathematics as a professor in one of the German universities. If we could see or converse with one of her pupils, and hear what they think of her, we should be able to form a better judgment than from all that her books and her enemies say for or against her.

I say her books, not her friends and enemies, for I fear she has no friends to plead for her except her books. I never met any one of any party who was her friend. This strikes me with real melancholy, to see a woman of the first talents in Europe, who had lived and shone in the gay court of the gayest nation in the world, now deserted and forlorn, living in wretched lodgings, with some of the pictures and finery—the wreck of her fortunes—before her eyes; without society, without a single friend, admired—and despised. She lived literally in spite, not in pity. Her cruelty in drawing a profligate character of the queen, after her execution, in *Les Chevaliers du Cigne*; her taking her pupils at the beginning of the Revolution to the revolutionary clubs; her connection with the late Duke of Orleans, and her hypocrisy about it; her insisting on being governess to his children when the duchess did not wish it, and its being supposed that it was she who instigated the duke in all his horrible conduct; and, more than all the rest, her own attacks and apologies, have brought her into all this isolated state of reprobation. And now, my dear aunt, I have told you all I know, or have heard or think about her; and perhaps I have tired you, but I fancied that it was a subject particularly interesting to you; and if I have been mistaken you will, with your usual good nature, forgive me and say, "I am sure Maria meant it kindly."

While at Paris, at the mature age of thirty-six, there happened to Miss Edgeworth what is said to be the most important episode in a woman's life— she fell in love. The object of her affections was a M. Edelcrantz, a Swede, private secretary to the King, whose strong, spirited character and able conversation attracted her greatly. She had not, however, reasoned concerning her feelings, and never realized either how strong they were, or dreamed that they would be reciprocated. Knowing herself to be plain and, as she deemed, unattractive, and being no longer young, it did not occur to her that any man would wish to marry her. While writing a long, chatty letter to her aunt one day in December, she was suddenly interrupted by his visit and proposal:—

Here, my dear aunt, I was interrupted in a manner that will surprise you as much as it surprised me, by the coming in of Monsieur Edelcrantz, a Swedish gentleman, whom we have mentioned to you, of superior understanding and mild manners; he came to offer me his hand and heart!!

My heart, you may suppose, cannot return his attachment, for I have seen very little of him, and have not had time to form any judgment, except that I think nothing could tempt me to leave my own dear friends and my own country to live in Sweden. My dearest aunt, I write to you the first moment, as, next to my father and mother, no person in the world feels so much interest in all that concerns me. I need not tell you that my father,

"Such in this moment as in all the past,"

is kindness itself—kindness far superior to what I deserve, but I am grateful for it.

A few days later she writes to her cousin:—

I take it for granted, my dear friend, that you have by this time seen a letter I wrote a few days ago to my aunt. To you, as to her, every thought of my mind is open. I persist in refusing to leave my country and friends to live at the court of Stockholm. And he tells me (of course) that there is nothing he would not sacrifice for me except his duty; he has been all his life in the service of the King of Sweden, has places under him, and is actually employed in collecting information for a large political establishment. He thinks himself bound in honor to finish what he has begun. He says he should not fear the ridicule or blame that would be thrown upon him by his countrymen for quitting his country at his age, but that he would despise himself if he abandoned his duty for any passion. This is all very reasonable, but reasonable for him only, not for me, and I have never felt anything for him but esteem and gratitude.

Mrs. Edgeworth supplements these letters in the unpublished memoir of her stepdaughter, which she wrote for her family and nearest friends. She says:—

Even after her return to Edgeworthstown it was long before Maria recovered the elasticity of her mind. She exerted all her powers of self-command, and turned her attention to everything which her father suggested for her to write. But *Leonora*, which she began immediately after our return home, was written with the hope of pleasing the Chevalier Edelcrantz; it was written in a style which he liked, and the idea of what he would think of it was, I believe, present to her in every page she wrote. She never heard that he had even read it. From the time they parted at Paris there was no sort of communication between them; and beyond the chance which brought us sometimes into company with travellers who had been in Sweden, or the casual mention of M. Edelcrantz in the newspapers or the scientific journals, we never heard more of one who had been of such supreme interest to her, as to us all at Paris, and of whom Maria continued to have all her life the most romantic recollection.

Miss Edgeworth's self-control was manifested at once. In none of her other letters does the matter recur; they are as chatty and lively as ever; but the incident throws much light both upon her character and the precepts of repression of feelings she loved to inculcate. She had not merely preached, but practiced them.

In January, 1803, Mr. Edgeworth suddenly received a peremptory order from the French Government to quit Paris in twenty-four hours and France in fifteen days. Much amazed, he went to Passy, taking Miss Edgeworth with him, and quietly awaited the solution of the riddle. It proved that Bonaparte believed him to be brother to the Abbé Edgeworth, the devoted friend of Louis XVI., and not till it was explained to him that the relationship was more distant was Mr. Edgeworth allowed to return. The cause for the order, as for its withdrawal, was petty. The Edgeworths' visit was, however, after all, brought to an abrupt conclusion. Rumors of imminent hostilities began to be heard, and though the reports circulated were most contradictory, Mr. Edgeworth thought it wise to be ready for departure. It was decided that M. Le Breton, who was well informed about Bonaparte's plans, should, at a certain evening party, give Mr. Edgeworth a hint, and, as he dared neither speak nor write, he was suddenly to put on his hat if war were probable. The hat was put on, and Mr. Edgeworth and his family hurried away from Paris. They were but just in time. Mr. Lovell Edgeworth, who was on his way from Geneva, and never received his father's warning letter, was stopped on his journey, made prisoner, and remained among the *détenus* till 1814.

After a short stay in London the family went to Edinburgh to visit Henry Edgeworth, who had shown signs of the family malady. Here they spent an agreeable time, seeing the many men of learning who in those days made Edinburgh a delightful residence. Warm friendships were formed with the Alisons, the Dugald Stewarts, and Professor Playfair.

Returned to Edgeworthstown, Miss Edgeworth set to work industriously to prepare for the press her *Popular Tales*, and write *Leonora* and several of the *Tales of Fashionable Life*. She exerted all her powers of self-command to throw her energy into her writing, and to follow up every suggestion made by her father; but it was clear to those who observed her closely that she had not forgotten the man of whom, all her life, she retained a tender memory. It was long before she thoroughly recovered her elasticity of spirits, and the mental struggle did not pass over without leaving its mark. Early in 1805 Miss Edgeworth fell seriously ill with a low, nervous fever; it was some while before she could leave her room, read, or even speak. As she got better she liked to be read to, though scarcely able to express her thanks. The first day she was really convalescent was destined to mark an era in her life. While she was lying on the library sofa her sister Charlotte read out to her *The Lay of the Last Minstrel*, then just published. It was the beginning of Miss Edgeworth's enthusiastic admiration of Scott, which resulted in a warm friendship between the two authors.

From the time of the Edgeworths' return Ireland had been agitated with the fears of a French invasion, and Mr. Edgeworth once more exerted himself to establish telegraphic communication across the country. As usual, his family joined him in his pursuits, and Miss Edgeworth, with the rest, was kept employed in copying out the vocabularies used in conversations. The year 1804 was almost engrossed by this. Nevertheless she found time to write *Griselda* at odd moments in her own room. Her father knew nothing either of the plan of the book or of its execution, and she sent it on her own account to her publisher, Johnson, with the request to print the title-page of a single copy without her name, and to send it over to Mr. Edgeworth as a new novel just come out. Miss Sneyd, who was in the secret, led him to peruse it quickly. He read it with surprise and admiration, and feeling convinced that Miss Edgeworth had not had the actual time to write it, and yet seeing it was like her style, he fancied his daughter Anna (Mrs. Beddoes) must have written it to please him. When at last he was told that it was by his favorite daughter, he was amused at the trick, and delighted at having admired the book without knowing its author. This was one of the many little ways in which the Edgeworths loved to please one another. A happier, more united household it would be hard to find among circumstances fraught with elements of domestic discord—the children and relatives of four wives, of the most diverse characters and tastes, living peaceably under one roof. Vitality, unwearying activity free from restlessness, distinguished most of its members, and especially the father and eldest daughter. Nor was there anything prim or starched in the home atmosphere; though ethically severe and maintained at a high level of thought, gaiety, laughter and all the lighter domestic graces prevailed. Miss Edgeworth's letters reflect a cheerful, united home of the kind she loves to paint. Like many united families, the Edgeworths were strong in a belief in their own relations; they had the clan feeling well developed. Not a member went forth from the paternal nest but was held in constant remembrance, in constant intercourse with home, and it was usually Miss Edgeworth's ready pen that kept the link well knit. Hence the large number of her family letters extant, many of which have no separate interest for the world, but which, taken as a whole, reflect both her own unselfish personality and the busy life of young and old around her. In her letters she never dwells on troubles; they overflow with spirits, life and hope. As they are apt to be long and diffuse, it is not easy to quote from them; but every one presents a nature that beat in unison with all that is noble and good. She was alive to everything around her, full of generous sympathies, enthusiastic in her admiration of all that had been achieved by others. Her praises came fresh and warm from a warm and eloquent Irish heart. That these utterances are toned down and tamed in her books, is yet another proof how the need to illustrate her father's ulterior aims cramped her in the expression of her feelings. His mind, though she knew it not, was inferior to hers, and though it was in some respects like her own, it yet hung heavy on the wings of her fancy. In later life she wrote more letters to acquaintances than at this time. In these years she says to a friend who upbraided her for not writing oftener:—

I do not carry on what is called a regular correspondence with anybody except with one or two of my very nearest relations. And it is best to tell you the plain truth, that my father particularly dislikes to see me writing letters; therefore I write as few as I possibly can.

Of herself she speaks least of all, of her writings seldom, and when she does, but incidentally. Without certainly intending it, she painted herself when she writes of Mrs. Emma Granby ("the modern Griselda"):—

All her thoughts were intent upon making her friends happy. She seemed to live in them more than in herself, and from sympathy rose the greatest pleasure and pain of her existence. Her sympathy was not of that useless kind which is called forth only by the elegant fictitious sorrows of a heroine of romance; hers was ready for all the occasions of real life; nor was it to be easily checked by the imperfections of those to whom she could be of service.

It is one of the most delightful features in Miss Edgeworth, that in her the dignity of the author is sustained by the moral worth of the individual—a combination unhappily not common.

Visits to and from neighbors or friends, more or less eminent, visits from nephews and nieces, letters from all quarters of the globe, prevented the life at Edgeworthstown from ever becoming stagnant, even if a home so full of young people could be devoid of life. Then, too, though the Edgeworths kept themselves aloof from politics, the course of public affairs did not always hold aloof from them, and at various times the disturbed state of Ireland caused them discomfort and fears. Sorrows and sickness, too, did not refrain from entering that happy home. There were the usual juvenile illnesses, there were births, there were sicknesses among the elder branches. In 1807 Charlotte, the darling of the family, died after much suffering, a victim to hereditary consumption. In 1809 Mr. Edgeworth himself was seriously ill, and Henry's health, too, became so precarious that it was needful to send him to Madeira. For a long time it seemed likely that Miss Edgeworth would go out to nurse him, but the project fell to the ground; and a few years later this brother, her especial nursling, also died of pulmonary disease.

The sorrow for Charlotte's death cast a cloud over all the year 1807. During its course Miss Edgeworth's greatest pleasure was the planting of a new garden her father had laid out for her near her own room, that had been enlarged and altered, together with some alterations to the main building. She was at all times an enthusiastic gardener, finding pleasure and health in the pursuit. "My garden adds very much to my happiness, especially as Honora and all the children have shares in it." Then, too, Miss Edgeworth was kept constantly employed attending to the affairs of the tenants; no rapid, easy or routine task in Ireland. Thus she writes on one occasion:—

This being May day, one of the wettest I have ever seen, I have been regaled, not with garlands of May flowers, but with the legal pleasures of the season. I have heard nothing but giving notices to quit, taking possession, ejectments, flittings, etc. What do you think of a tenant who took one of the nice new houses in this town, and left it with every lock torn off the doors, and with a large stone, such as John Langan[8] could not lift, driven actually through the boarded floor of the parlor? The brute, however, is rich; and if he does not die of whiskey before the law can get its hand into his pocket, he will pay for this waste.

No wonder she once sighs, "I wish I had time to write some more *Early Lessons*, or to do half the things I wish to do." With the calls on her time, domestic, philanthropic and social, it is only amazing that she wrote so much. Her method of working is described by herself in some detail. From its very nature it could not fail to induce a certain stiffness and over-anxious finish. She says:—

Whenever I thought of writing anything I always told my father my first rough plans; and always, with the instinct of a good critic, he used to fix immediately upon that which would best answer the purpose. "Sketch that, and show it to me." The words, from the experience of his sagacity, never failed to inspire me with hope of success. It was then sketched. Sometimes, when I was fond of a particular part, I used to dilate on it in the sketch; but to this he always objected. "I don't want any of your painting—none of your drapery! I can imagine all that. Let me see the bare skeleton."

It seemed to me sometimes impossible that he could understand the very slight sketches I made; when, before I was conscious that I had expressed this doubt in my countenance, he always saw it.

"Now, my dear little daughter, I know, does not believe that I understand her." Then he would, in his own words, fill up my sketch, paint the description, or represent the character intended, with such life, that I was quite convinced he not only seized the ideas, but that he saw with the prophetic eye of taste the utmost that could be made of them. After a sketch had his approbation, he would not see the filling up till it had been worked upon for a week or fortnight, or till the first thirty or forty pages were written; then they were read to him, and if he thought them going on tolerably well, the pleasure in his eyes, the approving sound of his voice, even without the praise he so warmly bestowed, were sufficient and delightful incitements to "go on and finish." When he thought that there was spirit in what was written, but that it required, as it often did, great correction, he would say: "Leave that to me; it is my business to cut and correct, yours to write on." His skill in cutting, his decision in criticism, was peculiarly useful to me. His ready invention and infinite resource, when I had run myself into difficulties, never failed to extricate me at my utmost need. It was the happy experience of this, and my consequent reliance on his ability, decision and perfect honesty, that relieved me from the vacillation and anxiety to which I was so much subject, that I am sure I should not have written or finished anything without his support. He inspired in my mind a degree of hope and confidence, essential in the first instance to the full exertion of the mental powers, and necessary to insure perseverance in any occupation. Such, happily for me, was his power over my mind, that no one thing I ever began to write was ever left unfinished.

That such a process was calculated to check inspiration is obvious. To suffer one hand to chisel and clip the productions of another, to insert into a finished frame-work incongruous episodes intended to work out a pet idea, was as inartistic as it was pernicious. The method could not fail to induce a certain self-consciousness on the part of the writer fatal to spontaneity, a certain complacent, careful laying out of plans, apt to disturb if not to distract the reader by drawing his attention from the fabric to the machinery. It was this that laid Miss Edgeworth open to the charge, so often made, of a mechanical spirit in her writings. For our own part, after reading her letters, with which her father certainly did not meddle, we are inclined to lay most of her faults to the charge of the monitor and guide whose assistance she so much over-rated. He, on the other hand, saw other dangers in their system. Writing to Mrs. Inchbald, he says:—

Maria has one great disadvantage in this house—she has eight or nine auditors who are no contemptible judges of literature, to whom she reads whatever she intends to publish. Now, she reads and acts so admirably well, that she can make what is really dull appear to be lively.

Indeed, everything was done in public in that family. All Miss Edgeworth's works were written in the common sitting-room, with the noise of playing children about her. Her early habits of abstraction stood her in good stead, and, at her little table by the fire, she would sit for half an hour together, without stirring, with her pen in her hand, or else scribble away very fast in the neat writing that never altered to the end. A certain occasional want of closeness in her reasoning may perhaps, however, have resulted from this habit of writing in public, since the effort of abstraction made by the brain must of necessity absorb some of its power. Considering how large was the family continually around her, it is sufficiently astonishing that she could do it at all. Once when such surprise was expressed, Mrs. Edgeworth said: "Maria was always the same; her mind was so rightly balanced, everything was so honestly weighed, that she suffered no inconvenience from what would disturb or distract any ordinary writer."

CHAPTER VIII.

FASHIONABLE AND POPULAR TALES.

WHEN the literary history of the nineteenth century is written, its historians will be amazed to find how important a part the contributions of women have played therein. At the meeting-point of the two centuries it was Miss Edgeworth in Ireland, Miss Austen in England, and Miss Ferrier in Scotland, who for Great Britain inaugurated an era of female authorship that stood and sought to stand simply upon its own merits, neither striving to be masculine nor addressing itself exclusively to women. Fielding, Smollett and the older novelists were not solicitous about virtue. They wrote for men readers only, and if they amused, their end was attained. But when women became readers a new need arose, and with the need came a new supply. The finer ethical instincts of women were revolted by the grossness of the Tom Joneses, the Tristram Shandys of literature; and as society became purer, manners less coarse, men too asked for mental food that should be less gross in texture. Miss Burney had led the way to a new era, a new style, both in fictitious literature and in female authorship. It was in her footsteps that Miss Edgeworth trod; but while Miss Burney aimed at amusement only, Miss Edgeworth inaugurated the novel with a purpose.

Perhaps no phrase has been more misunderstood than this of "a novel with a purpose."

Obviously it is not only right but imperative that a novel, or any work of art, should have a leading idea, an aim; but this is markedly different from a didactic purpose, which is implied by the phrase. Readers of novels demand before all else to be entertained, and are justified in that demand, and they merely submit to such instruction or moralizing as can be poured into their minds without giving them too much trouble. Miss Edgeworth lost sight of this too often; indeed, it was a point of view that did not enter into her philosophy, narrowed as her experience was by the boundaries of home and the all-pervading influence of her father's passion for the didactic. The omission proved the stumbling-block that hindered her novels from attaining the highest excellence. A moral was ever uppermost in Miss Edgeworth's mind, and for its sake she often strained truth and sacrificed tenderness. She was forever weighted by her purpose; hence her imagination, her talents, had not free play, and hence the tendency in all her writings to make things take a more definite course than they do in real life, where purpose and results are not always immediately in harmony, nor indeed always evident. Miss Kavanagh has aptly said, "Life is more mysterious than Miss Edgeworth has made it." Having said this, however, we have laid our finger upon the weak point of her novels, in which there is so much to praise, such marked ability, such delicious humor, such exuberant creative fancy and variety, that the general public does very ill to have allowed them to sink so much into oblivion.

Between the years 1804 and 1813 Miss Edgeworth published *Leonora*, *Griselda*, and the stories of various length that were issued under the collective titles of *Tales front Fashionable Life* and *Popular Tales*. *Leonora* was the first work she wrote after her return from France, where she had enlarged the sphere of her mind and heart. It is a marked improvement upon *Belinda*, the fable is better contrived, the language flows more easily. It was penned with a view to please M. Edelcrantz, and in respect of being written for one special reader, *Leonora* recalls that curious work by Madame Riccoboni, *Lettres de Fanni Butlerd à Milord Charles Alfred*, published as a fiction, but in reality only the collection of the writer's love-letters to the Englishman who had wronged and deserted her. "Mistris Fanni to one reader," was the significant heading to the preface of that book.

Miss Edgeworth's purpose in *Leonora* certainly led her into an entirely new path. To use her own words, no one would have believed that she could have been such an expert in the language of sentimental logic. For her doubly romantic purpose she was able to argue with all the sophistry and casuistry, of false, artificial and exaggerated feeling that can make vices assume the air of virtues, and virtues those of vices, until it is impossible even to know them asunder. The story itself rests upon a narrow and not very probable foundation. Its great fault is that it is too long drawn out for its base. The principal characters are a virtuous, outwardly cold and precise, inwardly warm-hearted English wife, and a well-bred English husband, led astray by the machinations of a Frenchified coquette who sets upon him from pure *désœuvrement*, and for whom any other person who had come into her path at that moment would have been equally acceptable game. The work is thrown into the form of letters, which gives to Miss Edgeworth an opportunity, inimitably carried out, of making all the personages paint themselves and speak in the language that is most natural to them. These letters are excellently varied. Lady Olivia's teem with French and German sentiment and metaphysics of self-deception; Leonora's are as candid and generous as herself—yet though her motives are lofty, we discern a certain air of aristocratic hauteur; while the good sense in General B——'s is bluntly expressed.

The fault of the story is that the husband's conversion ought to have been brought about by purely moral means, and not by the accidental interception of his false mistress' letters. Thus the value of the whole moral is destroyed by its creator. That *Delphine* in a manner suggested this story, that but for this romance *Leonora* might not have assumed its peculiar shape, may be taken almost for granted. A certain notion of refuting this corrupt story, then at the high tide of its popularity, may also have been present in Miss Edgeworth's mind, who at no time was so much self-absorbed as to lose sight of the ultimate aim in all her writings. Those were the days of excessive sensibility, when to yearn after elective affinities was the fashion. From such a state of feeling Miss Edgeworth's temperament and training secured her, and for very fear of it she erred in an opposite extreme. But with the true artist's instinct she recognized that it was in the air, and she makes it the theme of a romance that holds it up not only to ridicule, but shows with relentless force into what abysms it may lead its votaries. Over this novel Miss Edgeworth expended much time and care; it was subjected to frequent revision, while her father "cut, scrawled and interlined without mercy." It is certainly polished *ad unguem*, as he rightly deemed that a book of this nature, devoid of regular story, must be; but it might have been cut down still more with advantage.

It is the peculiarity of Miss Edgeworth's novels, and may be accepted as their key-note, that she systematically addressed herself to the understanding rather than to the heart of her readers, and that she rarely forgot her educational aim. After having striven to instruct children and young men and women, she tried, in a series of tales selected from fashionable life, "to point out some of the errors to which the higher classes of society are disposed." It is an open question whether it is possible to correct society, or whether that is a hopeless task because society is too vain and silly to listen to words of wisdom. "England," said Mr. Pecksniff, "England expects every man to do his duty. England will be disappointed." Miss Edgeworth, however, who never doubted the value of tuition, attempted the task, and she was certainly right in so far that if it were possible to open the eyes of this class of persons, it would be by means of entertaining stories. Of course she only appealed to those who, though not gifted with enough good sense to go right of their own accord, are yet not past teaching, or too devoid of sense to be teachable, and she took immense pains to show how the greater part of our troubles in life arise from ignorance rather than from vice and incapacity. To teach the art of living, the science of being happy, is her one endeavor; and thus her fancy, her wit, her strictures, are all made to bend to her main purpose, that of being the vehicles of her practical philosophy. Yet to regard Miss Edgeworth as a mere teaching machine is to do her gross injustice. Like most people, she was better than her creed. Despite her doctrines, her genius was too strong for her, and it is thanks to this that sundry of these tales from *Fashionable Life* are among her highest and most successful efforts. They are also as a whole more powerful and varied than any of her previous productions.

The first series consisted of four stories: *Ennui, The Dun, Manœuvring,* and *Almeria,* of which the first is by far the longest. As is too often the case with Miss Edgeworth, the plot is clumsily and coldly contrived, the proportions not well maintained; but the work abounds with masterly delineations of character, and is a striking picture of the satiety induced by being born, like the hero, Lord Glenthorne, on the pinnacle of fortune, so that he has nothing to do but to sit still and enjoy the barrenness of the prospect, or to eat toffee, like the duke in *Patience.* He tries all amusements, but finds them wanting, and he would probably have been ruined mentally and bodily if a convenient catastrophe had not precipitated him temporarily into indigence and aroused all those better qualities of his nature and excellent abilities that lay buried and inert. It is not the least skillful part of this clever tale that it is told as an autobiography, the hero himself both consciously and unconsciously dissecting his foibles. Much of the scene is laid in Ireland, and gives Miss Edgeworth scope for those amusing collateral incidents, those racy delineations of the various classes of Irish society, in which she is still unsurpassed. She knew how to hit off to the life the several peculiarities of respective stations and characters, and we know not whom most to admire and delight in: the Irish pauper who officiates as postilion, and who assures Lord Glenthorne that his crazy chaise is the best in the country—"we have two more, to be sure, but one has no top and the other no bottom;" the warm-hearted, impulsive, happy-go-lucky Irish nurse, who has no scruple about committing a crime for the sake of those she loves; or Lady Geraldine, the high-born, high-bred Irish peeress, who speaks with an Irish accent, uses Irish idioms, and whose language is more interrogative, more exclamatory, more rhetorical, accompanied with more animation of countenance and demonstrative gesture, than that of the English ladies with whom she is contrasted. With inimitable skill we are made to see that there is something foreign in this lady's manner, something rather French than English, and yet not French either, but indigenous. Of course, rebels play a part in the story— it would not be a true Irish story without them, but, as usual, Miss Edgeworth dwells by preference upon the milder, more engaging aspects of the Irish character, upon their strange, pathetic life; and while not ignoring, brings into as little prominence as may be the frequent perjuries, the vindictive passions, the midnight butcheries, the lawless ferocity, the treacherous cruelty, of her half-savage compatriots.

The Dun is a short tale in Miss Edgeworth's most didactic and least happy style, dealing with a theme that should be more often emphasized and brought into view; namely, the unfeeling thoughtlessness of the rich, that withholds from the poor the result of their earnings, one of the most frequent and serious injuries perpetrated by the wealthy upon their indigent brethren.

Manœuvring is a detailed account of the machinations of a certain Mrs. Beaumont, a country lady, who expends a great deal of Machiavelism, left-handed wisdom and intrigue upon the projects of her children's marriages, and also upon securing to her family the fortune of an old gentleman who never had a thought of disposing of it otherwise. The mortification and defeats to which her circuitous policy constantly exposes her constitute the plot and the moral of the tale, which is not ill-conceived, and yet for some cause fails to interest us long.

In *Almeria*, Miss Edgeworth's admirable story-telling powers, her grace and shrewdness, are once more seen at their very best. It is the history of a woman who has sacrificed all the happiness of life, all the better instincts of her nature, for the empty ambition of being admitted into the charmed circle of fashionable society; and who, though she finds out in time that it is Dead Sea apples she has sought, has become so immeshed that she cannot break away, but leads an existence of pleasure-hunting, ever seeking, never finding that commodity, a warning example of

How the world its veterans rewards—

A youth of folly, an old age of cards.

The moral is not insisted on, but is allowed to speak for itself, and is on that account far more eloquent.

Except when dealing with Irish scenes, Miss Edgeworth is never happier than when painting the perverse or intriguing fine ladies of society, who, having no real troubles or anxieties to occupy them, shielded from the physical evils of existence, make to themselves others, and find occupation for their empty heads and hours, with results put before us so simply, and devoid of euphemism, by Dr. Watts. Well indeed has the proverb said, "An empty mind is the devil's house." In her kindly way Miss Edgeworth can be scathing, and she exercises this power upon women of mere fashion. The ladies of the period were less occupied with public and philanthropic schemes than they are now, and hence had more time to expend on follies and frivolities. The whole pitiful system of unreal existence led by these women is exposed with an almost remorseless hand, for Miss Edgeworth had no tenderness for foolish failings. Inimitably, too, we are made to see how then, as now, there was tolerated in fashionable society a degree of vulgarity which would neither be suffered nor attempted in lower life. It was just because Miss Edgeworth's lines were cast among the rich and idle that she was able to understand all the misery and heartlessness of the lives of a large section of this community. We see how their petty cravings, their preposterous pursuits, bring positive misery on themselves if not on others; how their dispositions are sophisticated, their tempers warped, their time and talents wasted, in their restless chase after social distinction, after the craze of being in the fashion. "The scourges of the prosperous;" thus happily have these giant curses of mere fashionable life been defined. Miss Edgeworth certainly understood fully the nature of the disorder of her patients, the *ennui*, the stagnation of life and feeling that devoured them and sunk many of them at last to a depth at which they no longer merited the name of rational human beings. At the same time (and this is a point which must be insisted upon) there is no sourness about Miss Edgeworth's pictures of good society; her pen, in speaking of it, is not dipped in vinegar and wormwood, as was the pen of Thackeray, and sometimes even that of George Eliot. Without snobbishness, without envy, she writes quite simply, and absolutely objectively, of that which surged around her whenever she left the quiet of Edgeworthstown and visited in some of the many noble houses of Ireland, Scotland and England, in which she was a familiar friend. That her pictures of contemporary society were correct has never been disputed. She reproduced faithfully not only its coarser and silly side, but also the more brilliant conversational features, that make it contrast so favorably with that of our own day, in which the art of talking has been lost. Lord Jeffrey, an authority, and one not given to flattery, says that Miss Edgeworth need not be afraid of being excelled in "that faithful but flattering representation of the spoken language of persons of wit and politeness—in that light and graceful tone of raillery and argument, and in that gift of sportive but cutting *médisance* which is sure of success in those circles where success is supposed to be most difficult and desirable." In support of his statement he points to the conversation of Lady Delacour (*Belinda*), Lady Dashfort (*Absentee*) and Lady Geraldine (*Ennui*).

The first series of *Tales from Fashionable Life* met with so much favor that the publisher clamored for more. Some were lying ready, others had to be written, but in 1812 Miss Edgeworth was able to issue a second series, containing three stories, of which one, *The Absentee*, ranks worthily beside *Castle Rackrent* as a masterpiece. The evils this story sought to expose came daily under Miss Edgeworth's observation; she beheld the Irish landed gentry forsake their homes and their duties in order to go to London and cut a figure in fashionable society, spending beyond their means, oblivious of the state of home affairs, and merely regarding their properties as good milch kine. How their unfortunate tenants were ground down in order to meet these claims they neither knew nor cared. Lord and Lady Clonbrony, the absentees, are drawn with vivid touches: she is devoured by ambition to shine in a society for which she is not fitted, and voluntarily submits to any humiliations and rebuffs, any sacrifices, to attain this end; he, uprooted from his wonted surroundings, cannot acclimatize himself to new ones, and, merely to pass his time, sinks into the vices of gaming and betting. Lady Clonbrony affects a contempt for her native land and pretends she is not Irish. As, however, she cannot rid herself of an Irish pronunciation and Irish phrases, she is constantly placed in the dilemma of holding her tongue and appearing yet more foolish than she is; or, by mistaking reverse of wrong for right, so caricaturing the English pronunciation that thus alone she betrayed herself not to be English. In vain, too, this lady struggles to school her free, good-natured Irish manner into the cold, sober, stiff deportment she deems English. The results to which all this gives rise are delineated with consummate skill and good-humored satire. The scenes that occur in London society are highly diverting, but the story gains in deeper interest when it shifts to Ireland, whither Lady Clonbrony drives her only son, Lord Colambre, whom she has sought to marry against his will to an English heiress. Unknown to his tenants, from whom he has so long been absent, and further purposely disguised in order to elicit the truth concerning certain unfavorable rumors that have reached his ears, Lord Colambre is a witness of the oppressions under which his tenants labor from an unscrupulous and rapacious agent, who feels secure in his master's absence, and in that master's indifference to all but the money result of his estate. Charmingly is the Irish character here described; we see it in its best phases, with all its kindliness, wit, generosity. There are elements of simple pathos scattered about this story. With delicate and playful humor we are shown the heroic and imaginative side of the Irish peasantry. We quite love the kindly old woman who kills her last fowl to furnish supper to the stranger, whom she does not know to be her landlord. On the other hand we are amused beyond measure with Mrs. Rafferty, the Dublin grocer's wife and *parvenue*, who, in the absence of those who should have upheld Irish society, is able to make that dash that Lady Clonbrony vainly seeks to make in London. Her mixture of taste and incongruity, finery and vulgarity, affectation and ignorance, is delightful. The dinner-party scene at her house would make the reputation of many a modern novelist. It was a dinner of profusion and pretension, during which Mrs. Rafferty toiled in vain to conceal the blunders of her two untrained servants, who were expected to do the work of five accomplished waiters, talking high art meanwhile to her lordly guest, and occasionally venting her ill humor at the servants' blunders upon her unfortunate husband, calling out so loud that all the table could hear, "Corny Rafferty, Corny Rafferty, you're no more *gud* at the *fut* of my table than a stick of celery!" As for the scene in which Lord Colambre discovers himself to his tenantry and to their oppressor, Macaulay has ventured to pronounce it the best thing written of its kind since the opening of the twenty-second book of the Odyssey. No mean authority and no mean praise! As a story it is certainly one of the best contrived, and the end is particularly happy. Instead of a tedious moral there is a racy letter from the post-boy who drove Lord Colambre, and who paints, with true Hibernian vivacity and some delicious malaprops, the ultimate return of the Clonbrony family to their estate, which, to the optimistic Irish mind, represents the end of all their troubles and the inauguration of a new era of prosperity and justice. For one thing, it is so much more in keeping that an uncultured peasant, rather than a thoughtful and philosophical mind, should believe in so simple a solution to evils of long standing; that what we should have felt an error in Miss Edgeworth becomes right and natural in Larry. The suggestion for this conclusion came from Mr. Edgeworth, and he wrote a letter for the purpose. Miss Edgeworth, however, wrote one too, and her father so much preferred hers that it was chosen to form the admirable finale to the *Absentee*.

What perfect self-control Miss Edgeworth possessed may be judged from the fact that the whole of the *Absentee*, so full of wit and spirit, was written in great part while she was suffering agonies from toothache. Only by keeping her mouth full of some strong lotion could she in any way allay the pain, yet her family state that never did she write with more rapidity and ease. Her even-handed justice, her stern love of truth, are markedly shown in this novel. She does not exaggerate for the sake of strengthening her effects; thus, for example, she does not make all her agents bad, as some writers would have done; indeed, one is a very model middle-man. She is always far more careful to be true than to be effective, she uses the sober colors of reality, she paints with no tints warmer than life. The chief and abiding merit of her Irish scenes is not that of describing what had not been described before, but of describing well what had been described ill.

Vivian was written with extreme care and by no means with the same rapidity, yet it cannot be compared to the *Absentee*. Here Miss Edgeworth was once more clogged by her purpose and unable for a moment to lose sight of it. "I have put my head and shoulders to the business," she writes to her cousin, "and if I don't make a good story of it, it shall not be for want of pains." It proved no easy task, and only the fact that her father so much approved it, upheld her. "My father says *Vivian* will stand next to *Mrs. Beaumont* and *Ennui*. I have ten days' more work on it, and then huzza! ten days' more purgatory at other corrections, and then a heaven upon earth of idleness and reading, which is my idleness." *Vivian* is a particularly aggravating story, so excellent that it is hard to comprehend why it is not of that first-class merit which it just seems to miss. Its aim is to illustrate the evils and perplexities that arise from vacillation and infirmity of purpose, and it is rather a series of incidents than one well-rounded plot. Miss Edgeworth loves to paint, not an episode in life, but the history of a whole life-career. This permits her to trace out those gradual evolutions of some fault of character in which she displays such consummate ability, such precision and metaphysical subtlety. The hero, Vivian, a man of good disposition, but lacking firmness of purpose, cannot say "no," while at the same time he has all the spirit of opposition which seems to go hand in hand with weak characters, and is by them mistaken for resolution. The faults, the errors, the griefs, this trait of character leads him into are the staple of the story, which ends mournfully, since Vivian's inability to cure himself of his fault finally leads to his own death in a duel. He has not inaptly been named "a domestic Hamlet." Like Hamlet, he is neither able to accommodate himself to life as it is, nor strong enough to strike out a new life on his own account. The tale abounds in clever pictures of aristocratic and political society, and is full of the intrigues, the petty meannesses of social leaders. As usual, the moral instances are both striking and amusing, reason and ridicule being mixed in those just proportions that Miss Edgeworth knew how to blend so happily. A serious defect is undoubtedly the fact that it is not possible to care for the hero, and hence we grow rather indifferent to his good or ill fortune, and after a while are weary of the undoubted skill and perverted ingenuity with which he apologizes for his vacillation. On the other hand, as ever with Miss Edgeworth, the subordinate characters are throughout excellent, drawn with force and life-like power. Lord Glistonbury alone would redeem the book from the possibility of being dull. This talkative, conceited man, of neither principle nor understanding, who chatters adopted opinions and original nonsense, who loves to hear himself speak, and believes he is uttering great things, is a distinct creation.

The story of *Madame de Fleury* is slight in texture. It relates the experience of a rich and benevolent French lady who conducts a school for poor children after the Edgeworth type, and is rather a transcript from real life than a tale. Formal and conventional though it is, however, it was never wholly possible to Miss Edgeworth to belie her genius. Invariably she introduces some character, trait or observation that redeems even a dull tale from condemnation. In this case it is the delicate skill with which is depicted the gradual decline in character of Manon, who from an unconscientious child becomes a bold, unscrupulous woman. It was in penning *Madame de Fleury* that Miss Edgeworth encountered the difficulty she had observed of making truth and fiction mix well together. *Emilie de Coulanges* is the too correctly virtuous and rather colorless daughter of a refugee French countess, whose provoking character is deftly depicted with its selfishness, its self-absorption, that renders her both ungrateful and regardless of the comfort of the English lady who has most generously entertained her at no little personal inconvenience. Unfortunately an irritable temper mars Mrs. Somers' good, generous nature, and causes her to weary out even the affections of those who have most cause to love her. It also renders her suspicious of the probity, the good intentions of her friends. She loves to arouse sentimental quarrels; the bickerings and ultimate reconciliation give her real pleasure, as a form of mental titillation, and she fails to see that, though with her it is all surface, as her real feelings are not aroused, this may not be the case with her victims. Mrs. Somers, who may rank as the true heroine, is a bold yet highly-finished portrait, conceived and executed in Miss Edgeworth's best manner.

The countess is little less happy. Miss Edgeworth possessed in a high degree that intuitive judgment of character which is more common in women than in men, and which, when properly exercised, balanced by judgment and matured by experience, explains the success they have met with in the domain of fictitious literature.

Again and again Miss Edgeworth proved the fecund creativeness with which she could delineate the moral and intellectual anatomy of the most varied and various characters. Her personages are animate with life and brightness. Above all else she was an artist in detail, and never more felicitous than when furnishing studies of foible in female form. Of this the *Modern Griselda* is a notable instance—a brilliant performance, almost too brilliant, for it scintillates with wit and epigrammatic wisdom; it never fails or flags for one little moment, so that at last the reader's attention is in danger of being surfeited by a feast of good things. The fable is the direct opposite to that of the old story of Griselda. In the words of Milton we are shown how it befalls the man

Who to worth in woman over-trusting,

Lets her will rule: restraint she will not brook;

And left to herself, if evil thence ensue,

She first his weak indulgence will accuse.

This the modern Griselda does to her husband's cost and her own. The story is a remarkable evidence of Miss Edgeworth's independence of genius. She showed no weak sympathy with the failings of her sex just because it was her sex, but, like a true friend, held them up to view and pointed them out for correction. Her objectiveness did not insure her, however, from misconstruction. Mrs. Barbauld wrote to her:—

I became very impatient for your *Griselda* before Johnson thought proper to produce it; need I add we have read it with great pleasure? It is charming, like everything you write, but I can tell you the gentlemen like it better than the ladies, and if you were to be tried by a jury of your own sex I do not know what punishment you might be sentenced to for having betrayed their cause. "The author is one of your own sex; we men have nothing to do but to stand by and laugh," was the remark of a gentleman, no less candid a man than Dr. Aiken: and then the moral (a general moral if I understand it right) that a man must not indulge his wife too much! If I were a new-married woman I do not know whether I would forgive you till you had made the *amende honorable* by writing something to expose the men. All, however, are unanimous in admiring the sprightliness of the dialogue and the ingenious and varied perverseness of the heroine.

To this letter Miss Edgeworth replied:—

Let me assure you that the little tale was written in playfulness, not bitterness of heart. Not one of the female committee who sat upon it every day whilst it was writing and reading ever imagined that it should be thought a severe libel upon the sex, perhaps because their attention was fixed upon Mrs. Granby, who at least is as much a panegyric as Mrs. Bolingbroke is a satire upon the sex.

Popular Tales were issued, and also in great part written, before the two series of *Fashionable Tales*, and, taken as a whole, do not approach them in merit. They are more crude in conception, more didactic in manner; the moral is too obviously thrust into view, and at times even the very philosophy the author strives to inculcate is halting. The intensity and severe restraint of her purpose had blinded her vision, perverted her logic; and thus the value of some of these ingenious apologues is lowered. There is a character of childishness and poorness about many of these tales that detracts seriously from the really accurate observation and acute knowledge of human nature that they inclose. Further, too, there is always such a sober, practical, authentic air about all Miss Edgeworth's narratives, that glaring inconsistencies and forced catastrophes strike us with double force as ludicrous and unnatural when introduced by her. We certainly incline to think that the result of perusing at one sitting the two volumes of Miss Edgeworth's *Popular Tales* could lead to that outburst of pharisaical pride:—

Said I then to my heart, "Here's a lesson for me!

That man's but a picture of what I might be;

But thanks to my friends for their care in my breeding,

Who have taught me, betimes, to love working and reading."

Popular Tales were devised with a view to correct the errors and temptations of middle-class life, and were intended for a class which in those days was not much in the habit of reading.

Mr. and Miss Edgeworth, though advanced and liberal thinkers in many ways, were conservative in others, and, curiously enough, carried the idea of class distinction into the domain of reading. They deemed that to reach the middle classes a different character of story must be conceived from that destined for persons of rank. There is a naïvete, a gentle absurdity, about this simple fancy that we cannot help attributing to Mr. Edgeworth's unimaginative mind. In a brief but bombastic preface this worthy personage sets forth the pretension of the writer of these stories, and gives a list of the classes for which they are adapted. Why did he not also devise some method, by which to insure that none of the tales should be read or bought save by persons of a certain social standard? It would have been equally reasonable. To make a distinction between tales for children and for adults is proper and right; to draw a fine distinction between classes, unfit and childish. The process of natural selection will of its own accord effect the result that no one will read that which is tedious. Yet even when hampered by the illustration of copy-book morality, Miss Edgeworth could not hide her power. She never repeats herself; every story is unlike the other. She does not angrily apply herself to the correction of the vices and abuses she holds peculiar to the class she addresses; neither does she magnify, even though she emphasizes. We only behold them shorn of the indulgences and palliations they too often meet with. She was neither a Utopian purist nor a sentimental innocent; nor can she belie a natural tendency to make her ethics rather a code of high-minded expediency than of high principle for its own sake only. Throughout her writings she shows that from low as well as high motives, good actions are the best; but she never suffers her characters to rest in the reward of a quiet conscience. Her supreme good sense was always mingled with a regard for the social proprieties; she never loses these quite from sight; her idea of right is as much to preserve these as for right itself. For, after all, Miss Edgeworth's life revolved amid the fashionable world, and lofty as her aims are, she was not wholly untainted by her surroundings. She accounts it no crime in her heroines if they look out for a good establishment, money, horses, carriages; provided always that the man they marry be no dunce, she will overlook any little lack of affection. But, after all, she was teaching only in accordance with the superficial philosophy of the last century, which led people to found their doctrines entirely upon self-interest.

Still, a tone of rationality and good sense was so new in the tales of Miss Edgeworth's period, that to this alone a large share of the undoubted success and popularity of the *Popular Tales* may be ascribed. Lord Jeffrey, criticising them at the time of their appearance, remarked that "it required almost the same courage to get rid of the jargon of fashionable life, and the swarms of peers, foundlings and seducers, as it did to sweep away the mythological persons of antiquity and to introduce characters who spoke and acted like those who were to peruse these adventures." Miss Edgeworth was certainly the first woman to make domestic fiction the vehicle of great and necessary truths, and on this account alone she must ever take high rank, and be forgiven if that which has been said of her in general be specially true of *Popular Tales*, that: "She walks by the side of her characters as Mentor by the side of Telemachus, keeping them out of all manner of pleasant mischief, and wagging the monitory head and waving the remonstrating finger, should their breath come thick at approaching adventures."

CHAPTER IX.

VISIT TO LONDON.—MR. EDGEWORTH'S DEATH.

BUSILY, happily, uneventfully time flowed on at Edgeworthstown, while abroad Miss Edgeworth's fame was steadily on the increase. But whatever the world might say, however kind, nay flattering, its verdict, this preëminently sensible woman did not suffer herself to be deluded by success. That she knew precisely and gauged correctly the extent and limits of her power, is proved by a letter written to Mr. Elton Hammond, who had over-zealously defended her from criticism:—

I thank you for your friendly zeal in defense of my powers of pathos and sublimity, but I think it carries you much too far, and you imagine that I refrain from principle or virtue from displaying powers which I really do not possess. I assure you that I am not in the least degree capable of writing a dithyrambic ode, or any other kind of ode. Therefore it would be the meanest affectation in me to pretend to refrain from such efforts of genius. In novel-writing I certainly have from principle avoided all exaggerated sentiment; but I am well aware that many other writers possess in a much higher degree than I do the power of pathos and the art of touching the passions. As to how I should use these powers if I had them, perhaps I cannot fairly judge, but all I am at present sure of is that I will not depreciate that which I do not possess.

Another letter to the same correspondent deserves quotation, as giving her views on authorship. Mr. Hammond had consulted her as to the advisability of his adventuring on that career. Miss Edgeworth replied:—

If everybody were to wait till they could write a book in which there should not be a single fault or error, the press might stand still for ages yet unborn. Mankind must have arrived at the summit of knowledge before language could be as perfect as you expect yours to be. Till ideas are exact, just and sufficient, how can words which represent them be accurate? The advantage of the art of printing is that the mistakes of individuals in reasoning and writing will be corrected in time by the public—so that the cause of truth cannot suffer, and I presume you are too much of a philosopher to mind the trifling mortification to your vanity which the detection of a mistake might occasion. You know that some sensible person has observed, only in other words, that we are wiser to-day than we were yesterday.... I think that only little or weak minds are so dreadfully afraid of being ever in the wrong. Those who feel that they have resources, that they have means of compensating for errors, have never this horror of being found in a mistake.

In the spring of 1813 Mr., Mrs. and Miss Edgeworth visited London, where they were much lionized. According to contemporaries it was the daughter for whom the attentions were mainly meant, though she, of course, deemed them intended for her father. Crabb Robinson said that Miss Edgeworth gained the good will of every one during this visit. Not so her father; his "cock-sureness," dictatorial and dogmatic manner gave much offense in society.

They met every one worth meeting during their brief stay, and many famous names glint across the pages of the one letter that has been preserved treating of this London visit. Perhaps it was the only one written, for she describes themselves as being, from morning till night, in a whirl of gaiety and sight-seeing, "that how we got through the day and night with our heads on our shoulders is a matter of astonishment to me.... But I trust we have left London without acquiring any taste for dissipation or catching the rage for finery and fine people." In this one letter there are, unfortunately, none of those delightfully detailed descriptions of persons and events that she gave from France. Among the distinguished persons she met, Lord Byron is mentioned. Singularly enough she dismisses him with just the last remark that one would have expected concerning the poet, about whose good looks, at least, the world was unanimous: "Of Lord Byron, I can only tell you that his appearance is nothing that you would remark." He, on his part, was more favorably impressed. He writes in his journal:—

I had been the lion of 1812. Miss Edgeworth and Mme. de Staël with *The Cossack*, towards the end of 1813, were the exhibitions of the succeeding year. I thought Edgeworth a fine old fellow, of a clarety, elderly, red complexion, but active, brisk and restless. He was seventy, but did not look fifty, no, nor forty-eight even. I had seen poor Fitz-Patrick not very long before—a man of pleasure, wit and eloquence, all things. He tottered, but still talked like a gentleman, though feebly; Edgeworth bounced about and talked loud and long; but he seemed neither weakly nor decrepit, and hardly old.

Byron then remarks that he heard Mr. Edgeworth boast of having put down Dr. Parr, a boast which Byron took leave to think not true. He adds:—

For the rest, he seemed intelligent, vehement, vivacious and full of life. He bids fair for a hundred years. He was not much admired in London, and I remember a "ryghte merrie" and conceited jest which was rife among the gallants of the day, viz.: a paper had been presented for the *recall of Mrs. Siddons to the stage*, to which all men had been called to subscribe; whereupon Thomas Moore, of profane and poetical memory, did propose that a similar paper should be *sub*scribed and *circum*scribed for the recall of Mr. Edgeworth to Ireland. The fact was, everybody cared more about *her*. She was a nice little unassuming "Jeanie Deans" looking body, as we Scotch say, and if not handsome, certainly not ill-looking. Her conversation was as quiet as herself. One would never have guessed she could write her name; whereas her father talked, not as if he could write nothing else, but as if nothing else was worth writing.

To turn from them to their works, I admire them; but they excite no feeling and they leave no love, except for some Irish steward or postilion. However, the impression of intellect and prudence is profound, and may be useful.

To the Edgeworths' regret they left London before the arrival of Madame de Staël, for whom all the world was eagerly looking. The poet Rogers, noted for malicious sayings, asserted at a dinner-party that this was not accident, but design; that Madame de Staël would not arrive till Miss Edgeworth had gone. "Madame de Staël would not like two stars shining at the same time." Fortunately, for once, he was reproved; for it happened that, unknown to him, Madame de Staël's son was of the company, who indignantly repelled the insinuation that his mother could be capable of such meanness.

As always, Miss Edgeworth was glad to get home again:—

The brilliant panorama of London is over, and I have enjoyed more pleasure and have had more amusement, infinitely more than I expected, and received more attention, more kindness, than I could have thought it possible would be shown to me; I have enjoyed the delight of seeing my father esteemed and honored by the best judges in England; I have felt the pleasure of seeing my true friend and mother—for she has been a mother to me— appreciated in the best society; and now, with the fullness of content, I return home, loving my own friends and my own mode of life preferably to all others, after comparison with all that is fine and gay, and rich and rare.

$$* \quad * \quad * \quad * \quad * \quad * \quad *$$

I feel that I return with fresh pleasure to literary work from having been so long idle, and I have a famishing appetite for reading. All that we saw in London I am sure I enjoyed, while it was passing, as much as possible; but I should be sorry to live in that whirling vortex, and I find my taste and conviction confirmed on my return to my natural friends and my dear home.

Seeing *Patronage* through the press, and writing the continuations of *Frank, Rosamond*, and *Harry and Lucy*, were Miss Edgeworth's immediate occupations on her return.

Early in 1814 Mr. Edgeworth showed the first infirmities of age, which resulted in a long and painful illness. During its course Miss Edgeworth's letters were only bulletins of his health. The anxiety the family had so long felt concerning Lovell Edgeworth, on whom, on Mr. Edgeworth's death, all his duties would devolve, and who was still a prisoner, was heightened by this event. It was, therefore, an increased joy when, upon the entrance of the Allies into Paris, after a forcible detention of eleven years, Lovell Edgeworth was at last released and able to hasten home. The pleasure of seeing him helped to restore his father's health; but it was evident that Mr. Edgeworth's constitution had received a shock, and he himself never swerved from the opinion that his existence might be prolonged a year, or even two, but that permanent recovery was out of all question. This did not depress him. As before, he continued to be actively employed, interested in all new things, in all the life about him, and repeatedly exclaimed, "How I enjoy my existence!" "He did not for his own sake desire length of life," says his daughter, "but it was his prayer that his mind might not decay before his body." He assured his friends that as far as this might be allowed to depend on his own watchful care over his understanding and his temper, he would preserve himself through the trials of sickness and suffering to the last, such as they could continue to respect and love. This assurance he faithfully redeemed, by dint of a self-control and a regard for the comfort of others that cannot be too much commended, and which of itself alone would win pardon for many of his irritating faults.

Waverley had just appeared, and every one was reading and discussing it. Scott, who had always been an ardent admirer of Miss Edgeworth, and who said in after-years that he should in all likelihood never have thought of a Scotch novel had he not read Maria Edgeworth's exquisite pieces of Irish character, had desired his publisher to send her a copy on its first appearance, inscribed, "From the Author." She had, however, not yet received this copy when late one night, after having finished hearing the story read aloud to her family, in all the first fervor of her admiration, she sat down to write to the unknown author. Mrs. Edgeworth, who had been the reader, relates that as she closed the volume Mr. Edgeworth exclaimed, "*Aut Scotus, aut Diabolus,*" and with these words Miss Edgeworth began her long and ardently-appreciative letter to the nameless novelist. All Miss Edgeworth's ready, generous, truly Irish enthusiasm breaks forth in this epistle, which is too laudatory, too much written *à la volée* to be truly critical. But Miss Edgeworth never was critical when her feelings came into play, or were allowed their course unchecked. She narrates to Scott how the story was read aloud, how when ended they all felt depressed to think that they must return to the flat realities of life, and how little disposed they were to read the "Postscript, which should have been a Preface." While she was writing her letter Mrs. Edgeworth opened the book again and noticed this chapter.

"Well, let us hear it," said my father. Mrs. Edgeworth read on. Oh! my dear sir, how much pleasure would my father, my mother, my whole family, as well as myself, have lost if we had not read to the last page! And the pleasure came upon us so unexpectedly—we had been so completely absorbed, that every thought of ourselves, of our own authorship, was far, far away. I thank you for the honor you have done us and for the pleasure you have given us, great in proportion to the opinion we had formed of the work we had just perused, and, believe me, every opinion I have in this letter expressed was formed before any individual in the family had peeped to the end of the book, or knew how much we owed you.

Your obliged and grateful

Maria Edgeworth.

To this letter Ballantyne replied; thus, even towards Miss Edgeworth, Scott kept up his anonymity. A little later she tells a friend: "Scott says upon his honor that he had nothing to do with *Guy Mannering*, though he had a little to do, he says, with *Waverley*."

The following winter was spent by the family at Dublin, for the sake of first-class medical advice for Mr. Edgeworth. That indefatigable, active-minded old man meantime, though far from well, made experiments on wheel carriages and published a report. There was much gaiety and some interesting society to enliven the winter, but nothing worthy of note is recorded by Miss Edgeworth. Anxiety on account of her beloved father was uppermost in her mind, yet she continued to write, and was busy upon some plays and upon preparing a third edition of *Patronage*. In this third edition she made some important alterations, changing the *dénouement* to gratify remonstrances that had reached her. She did not like this alteration, and doubted the propriety of making it after a work had gone through two editions. Her father, however, approved, and the public was more satisfied. There was certainly much that was unnatural in the previous course of the tale, in which the newly-married wife refuses to go abroad with her adored husband, but lets him go alone and remains with her father, who, it is true, was in grief, but who had another daughter to console him. This might be Edgeworthian, but it was not human nature; and the incident gave universal offense.

Every new book of value found its way to Edgeworthstown, and was eagerly read and discussed by the family. Miss Austen was soon an established favorite, while Mrs. Inchbald had long been valued. An occasional correspondence was maintained with her. Writing of the *Simple Story*, Miss Edgeworth says:—

By the force that is necessary to repress feelings we judge of the intensity of the feeling, and you always contrive to give us by intelligible but simple signs the measure of this force. Writers of inferior genius waste their words in describing feeling, in making those who pretend to be agitated by passion describe the effects of that passion and talk of the *rending of their hearts*, etc.— a gross blunder, as gross as any Irish blunder; for the heart cannot feel and describe its own feelings at the same moment. It is "*being like a bird in two places at once.*" ... Did you really draw the characters from life, or did you invent them? You excel, I think, peculiarly, in avoiding what is commonly called *fine writing*—a sort of writing which I detest, which calls the attention away from the *thing* to the *manner*, from the feeling to the language, which sacrifices everything to the sound, to the mere rounding of a period, which mistakes *stage effect* for *nature*. All who are at all used to writing know and detect the *trick of the trade* immediately, and, speaking for myself, I *know* that the writing which has the least appearance of literary *manufacture* almost always pleases me the best. It has more originality in narration of fictitious events: it most surely succeeds in giving the idea of reality and in making the biographer for the time pass for nothing. But there are few who can in this manner bear the *mortification* of staying behind the scenes. They peep out, eager for applause, and destroy all illusion by crying, "*I* said it! *I* wrote it! *I* invented it all! Call me to the stage and crown me directly!"

Mrs. Inchbald had written praising *Patronage*, but she had also found some faults. To this Miss Edgeworth replied:—

MY DEAR MRS. INCHBALD:

Nobody living but yourself could or would have written the letter I have just received from you. I wish you could have been present when it was read at our breakfast-table, that you might have seen what hearty entertainment and delight it gave to father, mother, author, aunts, brothers and sisters, all to the number of twelve. Loud laughter at your utter detestation of poor Erasmus "as nauseous as his medicines," and your impatience at all the variety of impertinent characters who distract your attention from Lord Oldborough. Your clinging to him quite satisfied us all. It was on this character my father placed his dependence, and we all agreed that if you had not liked him there would have been no hope for us. We are in the main of your opinion, that Erasmus and his letters are tiresome; but then please recollect that we had our moral to work out, and to show to the satisfaction or dissatisfaction of the reader how in various professions young men may get on without patronage. To the good of our moral we were obliged to sacrifice; perhaps we have sacrificed in vain. Wherever we are tiresome we may be pretty sure of this, and after all, as Madame de Staël says, "good intentions go for nothing in works of art"—much better in French, "*La bonne intention n'est de rien en fait d'esprit.*"

You will make me foreswear truth altogether, for I find whenever I meddle with the least bit of truth I can make nothing of it, and it regularly turns out ill for me. Three things to which you object are facts, and that which you most abhor is most true. A nobleman whom I never saw and whose name I have forgotten, else I should not have used the anecdote—the word which you thought I could not have written and ought not to have known how to spell. But pray observe, the *fair* authoress does not say this odious word in her own proper person. Why impute to me the characteristic improprieties of my characters? I meant to mark the contrast between the niceness of his grace's pride and the coarseness of his expression. I have now changed the word *severe* into *coarse* to mark this to the reader. But I cannot alter without spoiling the fact. I tried if saliva would do, but it would not. So you must bear it as well as you can and hate His Grace of Greenwich as much as you will, but don't hate me. Did you hate Cervantes for drawing Sancho Panza eating behind the door?

My next fact, you say, is an old story. May be so, and may be it belonged to your writer originally, but I can assure you it happened very lately to a gentleman in Ireland, and only the parting with the servant was added. I admit the story is ill told and not worth telling, and you must admit that it is very natural or it would not have happened twice.

The sixpence under the seal is my third fact. This happened in our own family. One of my own grandfather's uncles forged a will, and my grandfather recovered the estate my father now possesses by the detection of the forgery of a sixpence under the seal.

Thank you, thank you, thank you, for liking the two Clays. But pray don't envelop *all* the country gentlemen of England in English Clay.

Thank you, thank you, thank you, says my father, for liking Lady Jane Grandville. Her ladyship is his favorite, but nobody has ever mentioned her in their letters but you. I cannot believe that you ever resembled that selfish, hollow Lady Angelica. Would you ever have guessed that the character of Rosamond is like—M. E.? All who know me intimately say it is as like as possible. Those who do not know me intimately would never guess it.

Harrington came next. The idea of writing a story of which the hero should be a Jew was not her own, but suggested by an unknown correspondent in the United States, a Jewish lady, who gently reproached her for having so often made Jews ridiculous, and begged she would write a story that should treat of a good Jew. Scarcely was it finished than she began *Ormond*. In February, 1817, she read the first chapter to her father as they were driving out to pay a visit, the last Mr. Edgeworth ever paid. His health had become a source of grave anxiety, and though he masked all his sufferings with cheerfulness and touching unselfishness, it was too evident that his case was serious. The interest and delight he took in Ormond, and his desire to see the story finished, encouraged Miss Edgeworth to go on.

Her stepmother writes:—

In all her anguish of mind at the state of his health, Maria, by a wonderful effort of affection and genius, produced those gay and brilliant pages, some of the gayest and most brilliant she ever composed.... The admirable characters of King Corny and Sir Ulick O'Shane, and all the wonderful scenes full of wit, humor and feeling, were written in agony of anxiety, with trembling hand and tearful eyes. As she finished chapter after chapter, she read them out, the whole family assembling in their father's room to listen to them. Her father enjoyed these readings so exceedingly as to reward her for the wonderful efforts she made.

Enfeebled as he was by illness, and often while enduring pain, Mr. Edgeworth nevertheless continued as before to revise his daughter's manuscript with "an acuteness, a perseverance of attention of which I cannot bear to think," she writes in after years. "He would work at it in his bed for hours together, once at an end for six hours, during an interval of sickness and exquisite pain."

Thanks to the kindness of her publisher, she was able on Mr. Edgeworth's birthday (May, 1817) to put the printed volumes into his hands. It was the last book of hers to which he was to write a preface, and it was characteristic, like his others:—

In my seventy-fourth year I have the satisfaction of seeing another work of my daughter brought before the public. This was more than I could have expected from my advanced age and declining health. I have been reprehended by some of the public critics for the notices which I have annexed to my daughter's works. As I do not know their reasons for this reprehension, I cannot submit even to their respectable authority. I trust, however, the British public will sympathize with what a father feels for a daughter's literary success, particularly as this father and daughter have written various works in partnership. The natural and happy confidence reposed in me by my daughter puts it in my power to assure the public that she does not write negligently. I can assert that twice as many pages were written for these volumes as are now printed.

And now, indulgent reader, I beg you to pardon this intrusion, and with the most grateful acknowledgments I bid you farewell forever.

RICHARD LOVELL EDGEWORTH.

This preface was dated May 31st, 1817. On June 13th Mr. Edgeworth died, retaining to the last, as he had prayed, his intellectual faculties. His death was an acute grief to the whole family, a terrible, an irreparable blow to his eldest daughter. She was almost overwhelmed by sorrow, and during the first months that followed her father's death she wrote scarcely any letters. She had not the heart to do so; besides, her eyesight had been so injured by weeping, as well as by overwork the previous winter, when she had been sitting up at night, struggling with her grief and writing *Ormond*, that it caused real alarm to her friends. She was unable to use her eyes without pain; "the tears," she said, "felt like the cutting of a knife." On this account, as well as from her sorrow, the rest of the year is a blank in her life. In the late autumn she went to stay at Black Castle with Mrs. Ruxton, who cheered and nursed her. With rare strength of mind she followed the medical directions to abstain from reading and writing. Needlework, too, of which she was fond, was forbidden to her; she therefore learned to knit in order to employ herself. With patience, fortitude and cheerful disregard of self she bore the mental and physical sufferings that marked the year 1817 a black one in her life.

CHAPTER X.

LATER NOVELS.—GENERAL ESTIMATE.

FEW of Miss Edgeworth's stories were written quickly. In her case, however, the Horatian maxim was scarcely justified, for her best tales are almost without exception those written with a running pen. *Patronage* was one that was longest in hand, having originated in 1787 from a story told by Mr. Edgeworth to amuse his wife when recovering from her confinement. From her frequent mention of it, quite contrary to her usual custom, one may conclude she did not find it an easy task. In 1811 she writes: "I am working away at *Patronage*, but cannot at all come up to my idea of what it should be." We do not know whether it ever did, but whatever her verdict may finally have been, it is certain that *Patronage*, though one of the longest and most ambitious of her stories, is as a story one of the least successful. It is labored; art and design are too apparent; the purpose has too fatally hampered the invention. There is no denying that, while containing many excellent scenes, much shrewd observation of character, *Patronage* drags, and the reader is weary ere he has done. It is both artificial and common-place, and what is more unfortunate still, the whole fabric is built upon a confusion of premises. Its purpose is to demonstrate the evils that result from patronage, and to show how much more successful are those who rely only upon their own exertions. Both premises involve a *petitio principii*. A capable person helped at the outset may have cause eternally to bless the patron who enabled him to start at once in his proper groove, instead of wasting strength and time after the endeavor—often vain—to find it unassisted. Had she attempted to prove that it was better for each person to fight his way alone, because this was better for the moral development of his character, it would have been another matter. But this is not the line she pursues. There are no such subtle psychic problems worked out. The whole question is treated from the surface only, and the two families chosen to "point the moral" are not fairly contrasted. The Percys, the good people who shrink from help so nervously that they would rather do themselves harm than accept a helping hand, possess every virtue and capacity under the sun, while their rivals and relatives, the Falconers, have no resources but those of cringing falsehood. They are absolutely incapable, have learnt nothing, do not care to learn, and depend entirely upon finding a patron. They further rely upon their luck that, when settled in their various posts, no untoward accident may reveal their inability to fill them. Thus sound morality, good sense and an independent spirit are contrasted with meanness, folly and ignorance. As an eminent critic has well remarked: "The rival families are so unequal that they cannot be handicapped for the race. The one has all the good qualities, the other almost all the bad. Reverse the position; encumber the Percys (to borrow a Johnsonian phrase) with any amount of help; leave the Falconers entirely to their own resources; and the sole difference in the result under any easily conceivable circumstances will be that the Percys will rise more rapidly and the Falconers will never rise at all."

The materials of the fable, therefore, are not happy; neither, such as they are, are they artfully managed. The working out is bald, the moral bluntly enforced. Never was Miss Edgeworth more weighted by her aim, never were the fallacies of her cut-and-dried theories better illustrated. In this, her longest work, it is specially evident that her manner was not adapted to what the French call *ouvrages de longue haleine*. But if we at once dismiss from our minds the idea of deriving instruction from the fable, if we judiciously skip the dull pages of rhetoric or moral preachings that are interspersed, we can gain much real enjoyment from this book, whose characters are excellently planned and consistently carried out. *Patronage* contains some of Miss Edgeworth's finest creations. The Percys as a whole are

Too bright and good

For human nature's daily food;

but even in their family had grown up a character whom we can love, with whom we can sympathize—the warm-hearted, generously impulsive, sprightly Rosamond, who, according to her own testimony, resembled her creator. Caroline Percy is one of the very wise, self-contained and excellent young persons who so often appear under different disguises in Miss Edgeworth's tales. She is exactly one of those heroines to whom applies the wickedly witty remark put by Bulwer into the mouth of Darrell in *What Will He Do with It?* "Many years since I read Miss Edgeworth's novels, and in conversing with Miss Honoria Vipont methinks I confer with one of Miss Edgeworth's heroines—so rational, so prudent, so well-behaved, so free from silly romantic notions, so replete with solid information, moral philosophy and natural history; so sure to regulate her watch and her heart to the precise moment, for the one to strike and the other to throb, and to marry at last a respectable, steady husband, whom she will win with dignity, and would love with—decorum! a very superior girl indeed."[9]

There is also a certain family likeness in the good fathers of her books. They are, as a rule, preternaturally wise, circumspect, and apt to resemble Mr. Edgeworth. It has been well remarked that though we are told that a just man sins seven times a day, Miss Edgeworth's just heroes and heroines never fall. Undoubtedly there is a want of variety as well as of human nature in her good characters, but not so in her bad. There she ranges over so wide a field that we can but wonder whence she gathered all this vast experience. She owned a perfect mine of social satire, and the skill with which she drew upon it and shaped her various characters, so as to give them a positive personal interest and vitality, is astounding. She is equally happy in her villains, her fools, her fops; indeed, in painting these latter species Miss Edgeworth is unrivalled. She seemed to know every weakness and absurdity of which human nature is capable. The manner in which she holds this up to view is sometimes almost remorseless, as from the altitude of one who has absolutely nothing in common with such creatures. In *Patronage* we have several such. Inimitable are the two Clays, brothers, men of large fortunes, which they spend in all manner of extravagance and profligacy, not from inclination, but merely to purchase admission into fine company. They are known respectively as French and English Clay; the one affecting a preference for all that is French; the other, a cold, reserved, dull man, as affectedly denouncing everything foreign, boasting loudly that everything about him is English, that only what is English is worthy attention; "but whether this arises from love of his country or contempt of his brother" does not appear. If there is anything to choose between these two capital creations, English Clay is perhaps the better. His slow, surly reserve, supercilious silence and solemn self-importance are wonderfully sustained; but hardly less excellent is his brother, with his affected tones, his foreign airs, and quick, talkative vanity. Lord William is another remarkably well-drawn picture. He is an upright, honorable and enlightened nobleman, who constantly fails to do himself justice, because he labors under that morbid shyness known as *mauvaise honte*, so common in England, so rare out of her borders. The patron, Lord Oldborough, a high-minded, austere, but absorbingly ambitious man, is elaborated with much care and penetration. Very skillfully are we made to feel that his vices are rather those of his position than of his heart. Nor must Buckhurst Falconer be passed over, the only member of the Falconer family who has one redeeming feature. He once had a heart, and, though weak as water, and swayed by the low principles that prevail in his family, he cannot succeed in stifling every good or noble feeling, though he has striven hard to compass this end. These will crop forth occasionally, though they cannot stay his descent down the path of corruption. But they permit us to feel for him, to pity him; he is no cut-and-dried mechanical knave.

A book that contains so many fine conceptions cannot be called a failure, even to-day, and since Miss Edgeworth's contemporaries admitted her premises, it is no wonder that on its appearance *Patronage* achieved a great success. In those days, when novel-writing had not become so much of an art as now, the rapid downfall of the whole Falconer family within the space of a few weeks presented nothing ludicrous. Such incidents were familiar in romance, and held allowable there, even if known to be untrue to life. We now judge from the latter standard only, and reject, even in fiction, the improbable. In *Patronage*, Miss Edgeworth's fondness for poetical justice has certainly carried her very far. Here, as in other of her stories, difficulties are not allowed to develop and be overcome gradually, but the knot is cut in the most ludicrously childish and awkward manner, a summary catastrophe is imagined, so that the modern reader cannot forbear a smile. Still, *Patronage* remains a remarkable book, replete with sound sense, acute observation and rapid graphic illustrations of character.

Scarcely so *Harrington*. Here, as in *Patronage*, Miss Edgeworth had set herself to work out a moral, this time an apology for Jews. It was written to suggestion, and was on a theme that lay entirely outside the domain of her experience. She had to evolve a Jew out of her moral consciousness, and her delineation is as little successful as that of other writers who have set themselves the same task. Her zeal outran her judgment; her elaborate apology is feeble; and if the Jews needed vindication they could hardly be flattered by one of this nature, for she does not introduce us to a true Jew at all. Her ideas were based upon that rare and beautiful character, Moses Mendelssohn, a character as little typical of the Jewish as of any other race or religious creed, but common to all men who think and feel philosophically and have raised themselves above the petty prejudices of mankind. This was as much as to say that only a Jew who was no Jew was admirable and estimable. And even his daughter Berenice, whom we are led to regard throughout as a Jewess, is finally discovered to have been born of a Christian mother and christened in her youth, so that her lover, Harrington, can marry her without any sacrifice to his social and racial prejudices. This is weak indeed, since the whole purpose of the story was to overcome the baseless dislike Harrington had from childhood entertained for the mere name of Jew. It would, therefore, have been far more to the purpose had his prejudices been really, and not apparently, overcome. The truth is that Miss Edgeworth herself was a lady not free from prejudices; and a regard for the opinion of the world, for birth and social station, was one of these. At the eleventh hour she probably could not reconcile herself to letting her hero, a man of good society, marry a Spanish Jewess; and since he had shown himself willing to do so, carried away by his deep and sincere feeling, she doubtless held that he had done enough, and so terrible a fate must be averted from his head.

The story could not and did not satisfy Miss Mordecai's requirements, though she accepted it as an attempt at making amends. But the authoress herself recognized in later life that her friend "had no reason to be satisfied with it, as the Jewess turns out to be a Christian. Yet she was good enough to accept it as a peace-offering, and to consider that this was an Irish blunder, which, with the best intentions, I could not avoid."

Contemporary opinion certainly treated *Harrington* as not one of the happiest of their favorite novelist's stories. Yet with all its palpable defects there is such an admixture of excellence that *Harrington* should not be left unread, even though we may regret that such capital figures, painted with such nice skill and delicate discrimination, should be imbedded in so puerile a tale. The characters are keenly and lightly drawn, standing out boldly and clearly. The jargon of society is once more successfully reproduced, as well as those fashionable ladies who hide the claws of a tigress under a velvet paw, and whose complex and shifting nature Miss Edgeworth understood so well and reproduced so faithfully. How she, with her simple, direct character, came to comprehend them so fully, is almost a marvel. But intuition of character was a forte with Miss Edgeworth and the grand secret of her novelistic success. Her truth of touch was remarkable. Lady Anne Mowbray is a perfect model of that mixture of feline grace and obstinate silliness which the world so much admires in its young ladies; while her mother's insignificance, which is not disguised by a stately, formal manner, is delineated and sustained to perfection. Lord Mowbray is yet another of Miss Edgeworth's marvelously acute portraits of a true man of the world, of an evil nature. This is concealed by a fair semblance and good manners, so that it is needful to know him well to guess at the villain that is hidden under this attractive disguise.

Miss Edgeworth is at her ease and at her happiest in *Ormond*. Here she is on Irish ground, always for her the best, where she moves with most *abandon*; where she casts aside for a time some of her cold philosophy, and allows herself to appear as the vivacious Irishwoman, which at heart she was. Ireland, with its long history of bloodshed and social disorder, had none of those romantic incidents to offer to the novelist that were to be found in the equally wild but more noble and chivalric history of Scotland. Hence Sir Walter Scott had an easier task to perform than Miss Edgeworth. The history of which he treated allowed of judicious and poetic gilding. It lifted into more romantic regions. Irish history has, unfortunately, never been elevating, soul-ennobling. It is too much the record of rebellious seditions and foolish intrigues, lightly entered upon, inconsistently carried out. Such a history could scarcely kindle romantic ideas and desires in the hearts of youth, as did Scott's pictures; and Miss Edgeworth did wisely in her Irish tales to leave history carefully on one side, and to deal only with the Hibernian character and the delineation of social manners. For many years the mere name of Irishman had been regarded in England as a term of reproach, and they figured as buffoons in all the novels and plays of the period. It was Miss Edgeworth who first came to the rescue of her countrymen, and she did this by no exaggerated praises, but by sympathetic yet true presentment. Her national story of *Castle Rackrent* had established for her a reputation as a relentlessly truthful writer. She had invested the tale with none of the poetical glamor employed by most historical novelists, who seek to hide from sight the ugly sores that exist in the society they depict, and thus endeavor to make us deem that those good old times of which they write had, despite their lawlessness, some power and strength of goodness unknown to us. Miss

Edgeworth was too realistic a portrait painter to employ such methods; hence, where Sir Walter Scott's rich imagination led him at times astray, she, on her part, was often hampered for want of that faculty. Still, her very reserve was fortunate, considering the theme on which it was exercised, as matters Irish have for some cause never been treated with judicial calmness. Hence to no writer are the Irish so much indebted. Their less judicious friends were satisfied with indignantly repelling the charges made against them, while national partiality magnified all their gifts. Miss Edgeworth felt with them, loved them, but she was not blinded by her affection. Starting from the assumption that the prejudices which existed against her countrymen arose from imperfect acquaintance with them, she candidly presented them just as they were, with both their virtues and vices unvarnished.

After *Castle Rackrent*, *Ormond* was certainly the finest effort of Miss Edgeworth's genius, and it is scarcely fanciful to believe that it owes some of its excellence to the influence exerted upon her mind by *Waverley*. Had she but had Scott's eye for nature, and introduced us to some of the beautiful scenery in which her story occurs, the book might worthily rank beside any of the Scotch Waverley novels. Was it owing to Scott's influence, also, that we have in this case a less obtrusive moral?

The story of *Ormond* is in some respects the reverse of *Vivian*. The hero possesses innate force of character, and we watch in his career the progress of a mind that has not been cultivated, but shows itself capable of being educated by circumstances. Ormond is one of those persons in whom native intuition takes the place of instruction, and who of their proper strength are equal to all emergencies. The complications of the story arise from these inward propensities of his nature and the contending influences from without with which he has to grapple. He was an orphan who had been adopted by Sir Ulick O'Shane, but had not been educated, because Sir Ulick deemed that there was no use giving him the education of a landed gentleman when he was not likely to have an estate. An unfortunate difference with Sir Ulick's wife obliged Ormond to leave his guardian's roof and avail himself of the hospitality of a cousin, Cornelius O'Shane, who called himself King of the Black Islands, after his estate. More familiarly this original is spoken of as King Corny. Besides being one of the most delightful creations in romantic literature, he is an instructive study towards the comprehension of the Irish character. Macaulay pointed out, in speaking of the aboriginal aristocracy of Ireland, that Miss Edgeworth's King Corny belonged to a later and much more civilized generation, but added that "whoever has studied that admirable portrait can form some notion of what King Corny's great-grandfather must have been like." King Corny is a most genuine character; there is no nonsense, no false reticence about him; he is hasty and violent at times, but he is not ashamed to show it, neither does he hide his warm, kind heart. His frank and unsuspecting nature makes him adored by all his tenantry, none of whom would wrong their king. There is not a page in which he figures that does not furnish charming reading, and there is not a reader but will resent that King Corny is made to die so early in the book. It is all the more vexatious to have the most original and attractive figure thus removed, because it was needless for the due development of the story. That the interest, which certainly flags after his demise, is sustained at all is a proof that the story, as a story, is above Miss Edgeworth's average. And indeed, attention is well maintained to the end, notwithstanding a few most marvelously unnatural incidents that occur in the latter portion and stagger belief. They once more reveal Miss Edgeworth's curious clumsiness in getting her brain-children out of the difficulties in which she has involved them. The quick alternation of laughter and tears that is a marked feature of her Irish tales recurs in the earlier portions of the book, where the scene is laid in the Black Islands, of which Harry Ormond becomes "prince presumptive." The famous postilion's letter in the *Absentee* is hard run by the letter King Corny writes to Ormond when offering him his hospitality. Admirable, too, is the account of his reception by the single-hearted, generous, though eccentric monarch. This reception scene is characteristic of the primitive and somewhat dissolute manners of the time. Indeed, the whole of Harry Ormond's residence in the Black Islands affords Miss Edgeworth opportunities for exercising her peculiar felicity in displaying manners and customs. She does not present these by merely a few prominent and striking traits, but with delicate skill she insinuates little touches here and there that give local color and perfume to the whole. It is quite true that Miss Edgeworth's books bear reading twice; once for the general impression, the second time to see how cunningly this impression is produced.

Miss Edgeworth not having in the case of *Ormond* weighted herself with a text, we have hardly any of her "unco' gude" characters, but many of those mixtures that are truer to poor humanity. The exceptions are Lady and Miss Annaly, some of her monotonously similar pattern women, and Dr. Cambray, one of her dull and wooden immaculate men. Happily they appear but little in the story. The most able character, after King Corny, is Sir Ulick O'Shane, the political schemer and trimmer. A more vulgar or common-place writer would have represented him as an offensive hypocrite. Miss Edgeworth does not paint him in repellent colors, but lets him reveal his baseness little by little, and rather against his will, until the final catastrophe presents him in all his native vileness. His easy and agreeable social manners, his gentlemanly mode of feeling and acting, due, no doubt, to a long inheritance of gentlemanly traditions, are shown with profound penetration. It is a part of Miss Edgeworth's power to evince how "great effects from trivial causes spring;" she makes us vividly realize all the circumstances under which her events occur. Thus we witness their development, instead of being only presented with the final results. This was rather a new departure in her day, when events finished, cut and dried, were alone considered worthy of note. In her conversations she shows considerable dramatic skill: they are enlivened not only by looks and gestures, but by what is often as significant, by moments of silence, by changes of countenance, by all the minor matters that distinguish spoken from written words. Neither in dramatic presentation of incident, nor in picturesqueness and vividness of character-drawing, has Miss Edgeworth ever touched a higher standard than in *Ormond*. The fact that it was written and sent to press so quickly, in order to gratify her sick father, proved in its favor. The result was that it was penned with more spontaneity, was less carefully worked up than either *Patronage* or *Belinda*, or even the *Absentee*, and consequently it reads more natural. There are fewer forced sentences, fewer attempts at pointed and epigrammatic writing. These epigrammatic sentences, which, with but few exceptions, are but half epigrams, are somewhat aggravating, especially if too constantly repeated, since they thus picture neither common nor uncommon talk. It is this tendency, carried to its highest expression in the *Modern Griselda*, that makes Miss Edgeworth's personages, while acting and thinking like real people, not always talk as men and women would. As a rule, however, her style is easy, finished, flexible, and at times racy, and while seldom rising to eloquence, never sinking to tameness. Now and then it is a trifle cold, and she is too fond of erudite or far-fetched illustrations. The conversation of her day was, to use the language of the day, "polite;" that is to say, slightly stilted, prim, and confined within narrow bounds, and that she reflected it is a matter of course, but, as a whole, she managed to keep herself singularly free from its worst features. Indeed, her work was really of first-rate quality, and if we read it without troubling ourselves about her ethical designs or expecting to find a cleverly-told plot, we cannot fail to derive enjoyment from it, or to comprehend why her contemporaries rated her so highly, though they, on their part, perhaps, valued her moral teaching more than the present generation, which does not believe in mere sermons as panaceas. Indeed, now-a-days, the fashion is too much to divorce art from didactic intention. In those days it was the fashion to over-rate the service works of imagination can render virtue.

It would be easy to bring forward testimony regarding the fervent admiration bestowed on Miss Edgeworth by her contemporaries. She certainly missed, but she only just missed, the highest greatness. Did Madame de Staël put her sure finger on the cause when she said, after reading *Fashionable Tales* and expressing her great admiration, "*Que Miss Edgeworth était digne de l'enthousiasme, mais qu'elle s'est perdue dans la triste utilité?*" Yet to preach utility was held by Miss Edgeworth as a duty; but for this she might perhaps never have written at all, since no pecuniary needs drove her to authorship.

And allowing for this moral strain in her works, and the blemishes that result thence, which compared with all she achieved are but trivial, in estimating her work as a whole, we may well afford to change what Chateaubriand called "the petty and meagre criticism of defects for the comprehensive and prolific criticism of beauties." We must not look for features such as she cannot furnish, any more than we should seek for figs upon an apple-tree. There are certain things Miss Edgeworth can do, and do inimitably; there are others entirely foreign to her sphere. Her novels have been described as a sort of essence of common sense, and even more happily it has been said that it was her genius to be wise. We must be content to take that which she can offer; and since she offers so much, why should we not be content? Miss Edgeworth wrote of ordinary human life, and not of tremendous catastrophes or highly romantic incidents. Hers was no heated fancy. She had no comprehension of those fiery passions, those sensibilities that burn like tinder at contact with the feeblest spark; she does not believe in chance, that favorite of so many novelists; neither does she deal in ruined castles, underground galleries nor spectres, as was the fashion in her day. In her stories events mostly occur as in sober and habitual fact. In avoiding the stock-in-trade of her contemporaries she boldly struck out a line of her own which answers in some respects to the modern realistic novel, though devoid, of course, of its anatomical and physiological character. She used materials which her predecessors had scorned as worthless. She endeavored to show that there is a poetry in self-restraint as well as in passion, though at the very time she wrote it was the fashion to sneer at this, and to laud as fine that self-forgetfulness, that trampling down of all obstacles, no matter of what nature, sung by Byron and Shelley. She permitted just that amount of tenderness which the owner could keep under due control. She had no taste for what was named the grandeur, beauty and mystery of crime. She seldom devoted her attention to crimes at all, but gave it to those minor virtues and vices that contribute more largely to our daily sufferings or enjoyments. The novels of her day were too apt to bring forward angels or monsters, and though she also erred at times in the former respect, yet on the whole she departed from it, and was among the first to strike out that path since so successfully trodden, especially by female novelists, and notably by George Eliot—that of interesting us in persons moving in the common walks of men. In her *Popular* and *Moral Tales* she was encumbered like a clergyman in his sermon, and hence a too solemn and rather stifling air of moral reflection is apt to pervade. That she overcame it as much as she did, that her novels are as attractive and readable as they are, is to the credit of her genius, which not even Mr. Edgeworth could wholly overlay and stifle, and she thus with few exceptions triumphed over that tendency to the "goody," from which it seems so difficult for works intended for edification to keep themselves exempt. Next to her children's and Irish tales she is most excellent in her studies from fashionable life. Her heroes and heroines moving in the dismal round of inanities, miscalled diversions, are portraits touched up with nice care in detail, with a keen eye for subtleties and demi-tints. She loved to expose the false and mawkish doctrines thought fit for women. Her fashionable heroines followed the sentimental teachings of Rousseau and Mrs. Chapone, and held that the highest mission of woman is to please, and that she should be not only excused but commended if she employed every art to compass that end. High-mindedness was a factor unknown or at least unadmitted in their philosophy; fashion governed all; to be in the fashion was the main object of their lives. Miss Edgeworth did not condemn this too mercilessly or from too lofty a platform. Her morality, though unexceptionable, is never austere; she allows and even sanctions worldly wisdom within certain limits; she was too much a woman of the world herself to set up Utopian or ascetic standards. To make conscience agree with the demands of polite opinion was admitted to be a desirable and important factor. After all, we are all more or less affected by the mental atmosphere in which we live; none of us can wholly get outside the spiritual air that environs us, and see things from different points of view; and Miss Edgeworth could do so less than many, because she was less highly endowed with sympathetic imagination. Thus her shortcomings are, in her case, more than in that of many others, the fault of her surroundings and education. For, placed immediately under Mr. Edgeworth's personal influence, his powers of suasion and plausible presentment, it was not easy to escape, and his daughter never questioned his final wisdom or desired such escape. In a critical reading of her books it is amusing to note how ever and again her father crops forth. Thus her heroes constantly ask what manner of education the young lady of their choice has received, because as "prudent men" they feel that only on this can they base their future hopes of happiness. And yet, strangely enough, with this absolute faith in the power of education is combined a belief that nothing, not even this almighty thing, can overcome the fact that if a girl be the daughter of a woman who has at any time forgotten herself, no matter how good the education may have been, no matter that this parent may have died at her birth or the child never lived beside her, Miss Edgeworth's heroes regard her as necessarily lost—consider that it is impossible she should continue in the straight path. They will stifle their strongest feelings; make themselves and the girl miserable rather than marry her. A special instance of this occurs in the *Absentee*, where Lord Colambre prefers to break off his engagement with his adored cousin, the charming and high-spirited Grace Nugent, rather than wed her after he hears a rumor that her mother has not been legally married to her father. Hence a *deus ex machina* has to be evoked, who, like all such gods, cuts the Gordian knot in bungling fashion. After attributing all possibilities to education, there is quite a comic inconsistency in this method of visiting the offenses of the wrong-doer upon the victim.

But Miss Edgeworth, or rather her father, appeared to have no comprehension of the fact that misfortunes of birth most frequently act on the children as a deterrent; so that they make, as it were, hereditary expiation. But here appears the want of tenderness in Miss Edgeworth's work—a quantity she owned as a woman and lacked as an author. The two were certainly curiously different at times. But though not tender, she is always amiable and kindly, even though she does not look far beneath the surface and never deals with the soul. Unknown to her were its silent tragedies, its conflicts, hopes and fears. Those feelings that did not manifest themselves in life or action were beyond her range of comprehension. She had a genius for observing such things as can be observed; the lower depths are never stirred by herself or her characters. But it was her genius for observation, her power for reproducing what she had seen, that made her greatness—a greatness limited in its extent, but none the less greatness of its kind. Her works fully merit the admiration they have so long enjoyed.

An amusing summing-up of Miss Edgeworth's novels is given by Leigh Hunt in his poem, *Blue Stocking Revels*. Apollo gives a ball to all the eminent contemporary authoresses, and criticises his guests as they enter.

At the sight of Miss Edgeworth he says:

"Here comes one

As sincere and kind as lives under the sun;

Not poetical, eh? nor much given to insist

On utilities not in utility's list.

(Things nevertheless without which the large heart

Of my world would but play a poor husk of a part.)

But most truly within her own sphere sympathetic,

And that's no mean help towards the practic-poetic."

Then smiling, he said a most singular thing—

He thanked her for making him "saving of string!"

But for fear she should fancy he did not approve her in

Matters more weighty, praised her *Manœuvring*.

A book which, if aught could pierce craniums so dense,

Might supply cunning folks with a little good sense.

"And her Irish" (he added), "poor souls! so impressed him,

He knew not if most they amused or distressed him."

And now finally we are confronted with the question, will Miss Edgeworth's works live, or will they be left to grow dusty upon the library-shelves, in company with many names much respected in their day? Who shall say? The novel is, of its very essence, the most ephemeral style of literature, since it deals with the ever-shifting pictures of its time. Nor is this unjust. The novelist of worth receives, as a rule, his meed of recognition in his life-time, which is not the lot of writers in all branches of literature. On the other hand, to the student of manners, novels have a value no historian can outvie, and on this account alone Miss Edgeworth's should not be left unread. But not only on this account, for it is perhaps just in this direction that they err somewhat; for though no doubt true pictures of one section of society, there is no denying that Miss Edgeworth's outlook is not catholic; that the world, as she saw it, was prescribed almost exclusively within the bounds of so-called "good society"—a circle in which the heights and depths of life and feeling are rarely touched, because of the conventional boundaries within which its inmates are cooped.

Whence, then, the undeniable fact that Miss Edgeworth has gradually grown to join that band of authors known as standard, who are more spoken of than read? There is so much in her mode of life-conception that is entirely modern, so much that is in keeping rather with the advanced school of utilitarian ethicists than with the more sentimental school of her day, that it certainly does appear puzzling why she has not better maintained her place; for it would be idle to pretend that she has maintained it such as it was in her life-time. It cannot be because her plots are ill-constructed. When at her best she holds attention notwithstanding. Nor does an author's power to engross us at all depend on his constructive faculty. Indeed, some of those writers who most hold their readers have distinctly lacked this gift, which often exists independently of fine novelistic qualities. In portions of her work Miss Edgeworth need fear no rivals. Why is it, then, that in attempting an estimate of her powers, while allowing to her first-class excellences, we have to deny her a first-class place, thus condoning, to some extent, those who leave her unread to turn to less edifying and admirable writers? Is it not because there is absent from Maria Edgeworth's writings that divine spark of the ideal that alone allows works to live for all time—that spark which it is given to many an inferior author to own, while it is here denied to a woman of great intellectual power? While preëminently upright, high-principled and virtuous, Miss Edgeworth's ethics are pervaded by a certain coldness and self-consciousness that irresistibly give to her good people a pharisaical character; an impression from which it is always difficult and at times impossible for the reader to shake himself free. Her heroes and heroines act with too little spontaneity; they seem to calculate and know too surely the exact sum total of ultimate gain that will, in a justly-ordered world, accrue to them for their good actions, their self-sacrifice and devotion. Her heroes are almost as calculating as her villains.

It is a severe test to which to put an author, to read all his works consecutively; but it is one that more surely than aught else enables us to mark his place of merit. If he can stand this trial he is decidedly above the average; if he issue thence triumphant he may without hesitation be pronounced among the great. Miss Edgeworth weathers this test very respectably; indeed it, more than all else, enforces upon the reader the great versatility she displays in character and situation. Yet it is just after such a perusal that the absolute lack of the ideal element is so strongly borne in upon us. As the thirsty mountaineer drinks eagerly from the first clear streamlet that meets him trickling down from the heights, so Miss Edgeworth's readers eagerly turn from her to some more spontaneous writer to quench the drought that this continuous perusal has engendered. Even in this prosaic and materialistic age the belief in blue roses is happily not wholly dead; and though we will not suffer the garden of a novelist to grow no other plant, because we know that one filled with blue roses only is out of nature in this terrestrial globe, yet, in a well-ordered parterre, we do require that the blue rose should also have its place. It is to novelist and poet that the cultivation of this rare and heaven-born plant has been entrusted. Miss Edgeworth knew it not. Neither by hereditary tendency nor by training had she made acquaintance with this wonder-flower, for whose botanical analysis Mr. Edgeworth would have searched a Flora in vain, and whose existence he would therefore stoutly have denied.

With "little stores of maxims," like Tennyson's faithless love, Miss Edgeworth, acting from the very highest motives, after careful and philosophic deliberation, at personal suffering to herself, in her printed words, preached down the instincts of the heart. She knew not that excellent as utilitarianism is in its place and sphere, there is something more, something beyond, that is needed to form the basis upon which human actions are set in motion. For the spiritual and divine element in man she made no allowance, and it was this that drew down on her, from shallow contemporary critics, that condemnation of want of religion, flung in a narrow, dogmatic spirit, that wounded her so deeply. Outwardly the Edgeworths conformed to the established faith, and though liberal in the sense of being wide-minded, they were not in religious matters advanced in thought. Indeed, they thought little, if at all, of the next world, finding full occupation for their minds in this. Miss Edgeworth was hemmed in by the visible; she did not seek to justify the ways of God to man; life was to her no riddle; if man would but act rightly, all would be well; she deemed that it is given into his own hands to do good or evil, to be happy or the reverse.

There was in her nothing of the poet and the seer; and by so much as she fails to speak to humanity in all its aspects, by so much she fails to take rank among the greatest teachers of our race. But with wisdom and good sense she recognized her limitations; she set herself a humbler but no less useful task; she carried out her aim faithfully and conscientiously, and by so much she too must be ranked among the good and faithful servants who do the work appointed by their Lord. And after all, is not the harmony of humanity best served by the free emission of the most diverse notes? Miss Edgeworth set herself to preach utilitarianism and the minor virtues. She succeeded; and in so far as she succeeded in that which she set herself to do, life was for her successful, and she was great.

CHAPTER XI.

VISITS ABROAD AND AT HOME.

LIFE at Edgeworthstown underwent no outward change owing to the death of its master. His place was taken by his eldest and unmarried son, Lovell, who sought to the best of his abilities to keep the house a home for his father's widow and his numerous brothers and sisters, an endeavor in which he was successful. Miss Edgeworth describes herself at this time as "quite absorbed in low domestic interests, of which only those who love home and love us can possibly bear to hear."

For some years after her father's death all she did was done as an effort, and more from a high sense of duty and from the thought that it would have pleased him who was gone, than from any inner desire to act. When the family after a short absence reassembled at Edgeworthstown, it required all her inherited activity of mind, all her acquired self-command, to enable her to keep up her spirits on reëntering that house in which for her the light was quenched. It was well for her not only that work was the purpose in life of all that family, that no drones were suffered in that household, but that her work had been planned for her by her father, and that in settling down to it she was obeying his commands.

It had been not only his darling wish, but his dying injunction, that she should complete the memoir of his life which he had begun and abandoned ten years previously. Why Mr. Edgeworth had written his life is not made clear, even by the preface, in which he attempts to explain the reasons that impelled him. The real reason was probably the excessive importance he attached to himself and his actions. It had always been his intention that Miss Edgeworth should revise and complete this memoir; but when he was dying he emphatically enjoined that it should be published without any change. This complicated her task, which she felt a heavy one. Excepting a few passages, he had never shown what he had written even to his own family; and when he was urged by them to continue it, he used to say he "would leave the rest to be finished by his daughter Maria." Almost before her eyes were recovered she set to work upon her pious duty. Her anxiety lest she should not do justice to the theme weighed upon her so greatly that she could hardly speak of the memoirs even to her most intimate friends. It is reflected in the touchingly helpless preface she prefixed to the second volume:—

Till now I have never on any occasion addressed myself to the public alone, and speaking in the first person. This egotism is not only repugnant to my habits, but most painful and melancholy. Formerly I had always a friend and father who spoke and wrote for me; one who exerted for me all the powers of his strong mind, even to the very last. Far more than his protecting kindness I regret, at this moment, the want of his guiding judgment now, when it is most important to me—where *his* fame is at stake.

To save her eyesight her sisters assisted her in copying or in writing from her dictation; but even so she was forced to use her own vision, and while busy with the memoirs she allowed herself little of what was now her greatest relaxation, writing letters to her friends:—

We are looking to the bright side of every object that remains to us, and many blessings we have still. I am now correcting what I had written of my father's life, and shall be for some months, so shall not write any letters of such length as this.

Bear up and struggle as she would, bitterly and painfully she missed the always kind and ready adviser, the sympathetic intellectual companion, who had stood by her side till now and aided her in every difficult task. She felt like "drifting over an unknown sea without chart or compass." Nor were her spirits or those of the family raised by outward events. Wet seasons had induced famine and typhus fever, and the tenants were suffering from disease and distress. Then, too, the family had their own private anxieties in the illness of William, Lovell and Fanny. They were all more or less delicate; most of them had inherited consumptive tendencies, and many months rarely passed without Miss Edgeworth having to record cases of sickness in those about her. These illnesses always absorbed her whole attention, called forth all her kindliness and unselfishness. She was ever the ready, willing nurse, the writer of bulletins to those away, the cheerer of long, sad hours of suffering. They were weary months, those early ones of 1818, and only in her affections did she find comfort. She writes:—

I was always fond of being loved, but of late I am become more sensible of the soothing power of affectionate expressions. Indeed, I have reason, although much has been taken from me, to be heartily grateful for all I have left of excellent friends, and for much, much unexpected kindness which has been shown to me and mine, not only by persons unconnected by any natural ties with me or them, but from mere acquaintance become friends.

In June she was able to announce: "I am now within two months' work of finishing all I mean to write; but the work of revision and consideration— O! most anxious consideration." She was still desirous of having the opinion of friends, and more especially she desired the opinion of M. Dumont. Hearing he was to stay with Lord Lansdowne, at Bowood, she yielded to the importunities of these friends and went there to meet him, taking with her her sister Honora. She was soon able to tell Mrs. Edgeworth that Dumont "has been very much pleased with my father's manuscript; he has read a good deal and likes it. He hates Mr. Day in spite of all his good qualities; he says he knows he could not bear that sort of man, who has such pride and misanthropies about trifles, raising a great theory of morals upon an *amour propre blessé*."

The change of scene was clearly beneficial to her. Once more her letters were filled with the anecdotes, the interesting talk she hears, accounts of which she knows will give pleasure to those at home. To give pleasure to others was always the one thought uppermost in her mind. "I am a vile correspondent when I have nothing to say; but at least I do write in some sort of way when I know I have something to say that will give pleasure to my friends." The whole character of the woman is revealed in these simple words. Among the good stories she tells from Bowood is one concerning Madame de Staël:—

Madame de Staël—I tumble anecdotes together as I recollect them—Madame de Staël had a great wish to see Mr. Bowles, the poet, or as Lord Byron calls him, the sonneteer; she admired his sonnets and his *Spirit of Maritime Discovery*, and ranked him high as an English genius. In riding to Bowood he fell and sprained his shoulder, but still came on. Lord Lansdowne alluded to this in presenting him to Madame de Staël, before dinner, in the midst of the listening circle. She began to compliment him and herself upon the exertion he had made to come and see her. "O, ma'am, say no more, for I would have done a great deal more to see so great a curiosity!" Lord Lansdowne says it is impossible to describe the shock in Madame de Staël's face—the breathless astonishment and the total change produced in her opinion of the man. She said afterwards to Lord Lansdowne, who had told her he was a simple country clergyman, "*Je vois bien que ce n'est qu'un simple curé qui n'a pas le sens commun quoique grand poëte!*"

From Bowood Miss Edgeworth paid some other visits, seeing many old friends, and among them Mrs. Barbauld and the Misses Baillie:—

Joanna Baillie and her sister, most kind, cordial and warm-hearted, came running down their little flagged walk to welcome us. Both Joanna and her sister have such agreeable and new conversation—not old trumpery literature over again, and reviews, but new circumstances worth telling apropos to every subject that is touched upon; frank observations on character without either ill nature or the fear of committing themselves; no blue-stocking tittle-tattle or habits of worshipping or being worshipped; domestic, affectionate, good to live with and without fussing, continually doing what is most obliging and whatever makes us feel most at home. Breakfast is very pleasant in this house, the two good sisters look so neat and cheerful.

Although she had met with much encouraging criticism in the matter of her father's life, she still hesitated to publish. "The result of all I see, think and feel," she tells her stepmother, "is that we should be in no haste." Down to the very business arrangements the book weighed on her. She had hitherto left all such details to her father; and her kind friend Johnson being also dead, she felt yet more undecided how to act. At every moment, in every detail of her life, she missed her father; but she was too brave a woman not to struggle with her grief, or not to adapt herself to altered conditions. Her eyes still caused her much trouble, and for nearly two years she was obliged to give them almost entire rest.

But for her patience and fortitude in following the doctor's injunctions, it seems possible she might have entirely lost her sight. As it was, a complete recovery took place; and though at times her eyes were weak, she was able to the end of her life to read, write and work with ease. At the end of the year 1819 she is able gleefully to tell her cousin that she must now make up for lost time and read.

"Now that I have eyes to read again, I find it delightful, and I have a voracious appetite and a relish for food; good, bad and indifferent, I am afraid, like a half-famished, shipwrecked wretch."

She read all the new literature of the day, and eagerly inquired among all her friends what they commended. Byron's *Don Juan* had caused much talk, but this did not attract her:—

After what you have told me, and after all I hear from every good judge of *Don Juan*, I never desire to see it. The only regret I feel upon the subject is that any pearls should be found, as I am told they may be found, in this intellectual dung-hill. How can the public allow this drunken, flagitious actor to appear before them, disgracing genius and the taste of his country? In Scott's last tales there are all the signs of a master mind, but now and then all the spasms in the stomach, for which I pity him. I am glad he is going to try some new scheme, for he has, I think, exhausted every variety of Scotch character.

It was not till early in 1820 that the memoirs of Mr. Edgeworth were completed. Having arranged that they should appear at Easter, Miss Edgeworth resolved to carry out a long-cherished plan, that of visiting Paris in company with her two young sisters, Fanny and Harriet. At one time it seemed as if political events were too unsettled to make this project advisable, on which account she asked her good friend, Dr. Holland, of Knutsford, to propose some other plans. Very significant is the remark she makes: "Observe that Fanny and I both prefer society, good society, even to fine landscapes or even to volcanoes." Finally Paris was pronounced safe, and they set out thither. It was on this occasion, when crossing to Holyhead, that she made her first acquaintance with a steamboat. She disliked what she called the "jigging motion," which, she said, was like the shake felt in a carriage when a pig is scratching himself behind the hind wheel while waiting at an Irish inn door. Her letters to her stepmother and sisters during this trip are frequent and detailed. At Paris they stayed some months, establishing themselves domestically in apartments in the Place du Palais Bourbon. "*Madame Maria Edgeworth et Mademoiselles ses sœurs*" ran their visiting-cards, which were soon left at the best Parisian houses. Many new friends were added to those they had previously made, and under the changed régime the connection of Miss Edgeworth with the Abbé Edgeworth became a passport to the homes of the old nobility. The circumstance that Miss Edgeworth was a most accomplished French scholar, speaking the language with as much ease as if it were her own, enabled her thoroughly to enter into and enjoy the society that was offered her. Her knowledge of French classic literature charmed her hosts and brought out all their best powers of conversation. Her ready sympathy and real interest won their hearts and induced many of them to tell her the sad stories of their adventures in the revolutionary days. But her intercourse was not confined to the aristocracy. Her hereditary taste for science brought her in contact with most of the distinguished scientific men of France, while literary society was, of course, thrown open to her. She noticed a great alteration in manners since their last visit:—

I should observe that a great change has taken place: the men huddle together now in France as they used to do in England, talking politics with their backs to the women in a corner, or even in the middle of the room, without minding them in the least, and the ladies complain and look very disconsolate, and many ask "If this be Paris?" and others scream Ultra nonsense or Liberal nonsense to make themselves of consequence and to attract the attention of the gentlemen. In 1803, under the First Consul's reign, when all freedom of discussion on public affairs was dangerous, and when all parties were glad to forget the horrors of the revolutionary days, conversation was limited to literary or scientific subjects, and was therefore much more agreeable to foreigners; now in 1820 the verb *politiquer*, to talk politics, had been invented.

As a foreigner Miss Edgeworth was enabled to visit at the houses of all factions, and she found much entertainment in hearing their opinions and diametrically opposite views. The Emigrants spoke of the Liberals with the bitterest detestation as revolutionary monsters; the Liberals spoke of the Ultras as bigoted idiots. One of these said of a lady celebrated in 1803 as a brilliant talker: "*Autrefois elle avait de l'esprit, mais elle est devenue Ultra, dévote et bête.*" While not sympathizing with the insolence of either party, Miss Edgeworth extracted some diversion and yet more moral reflection from all she saw. Writing to Dr. Holland after she had been an observer for some time, she says:—

Upon the whole, after comparing the society in Paris and London, I far prefer the London society, and feel a much stronger desire to return to London than ever to revisit Paris. There is scarcely any new literature or any taste for old literature in Paris. In London the production of a single article in the *Edinboro'* or *Quarterly Review*, the lustre, however evanescent, it casts on the reviewer or the author, is a proof of the importance of literature in fashionable society. No such thing in Paris. Even the Parisian men of science, many of them equal, some superior to ours, are obliged or think themselves obliged to turn statesmen, and sorry statesmen they make. Everything in Parisian society is, as it were, tainted by politics, and the politicians themselves seem to be mere actors. I could forgive all their violence and the noise they make, screaming always all at a time, if they were really actuated by patriotism, but it seemed all for effect. A few exceptions, of course, to prove the rule.

The more she saw of Parisian life, the more convinced she felt that the French required, if not a despot, at least an absolute monarch to reign over them. A brilliant and ready talker, Miss Edgeworth was also an able listener, and hence her society was much sought after, while the beauty, intelligence and excellent dressing of her sisters caused them also to be regarded as acquisitions in days when the Continent was not swamped with tourists, as it is now, and natives were therefore able to open their doors. A galaxy of brilliant and historical names pass across the pages of Miss Edgeworth's letters, and many a reminiscence she has preserved of them. Her accounts of the various parties to which they went are so vivacious and graphic that those for whom they were written must have felt as if they had been present too, and had listened to all the talk in which science, politics, literature and nonsense were mixed in happy proportions. Here is an account of an evening at Cuvier's:—

Prony, with his hair nearly in my plate, was telling me most entertaining anecdotes of Bonaparte; and Cuvier, with his head nearly meeting him, talking as hard as he could, not striving to show learning or wit—quite the contrary; frank, open-hearted genius, delighted to be together at home and at ease. This was the most flattering and agreeable thing to me that could possibly be. Harriet was on the off side, and every now and then he turned to her in the midst of his anecdotes and made her so completely one of us; and there was such a prodigious noise, nobody could hear but ourselves. Both Cuvier and Prony agreed that Bonaparte never could bear to have any but a decided answer. "One day," said Cuvier, "I nearly ruined myself by considering before I answered. He asked me, '*Faut il introduire le sucre de bettetrave en France?*' '*D'abord, Sire, il faut songer si vos colonies*'—'*Faut il avoir le sucre de bettetrave en France?*' '*Mais, Sire, il faut examiner*'—'*Bah! je le demanderai à Berthollet.*'" This despotic, laconic mode of insisting on learning everything in two words had its inconveniences. One day he asked the master of the woods at Fontainebleau, "How many acres of wood here?" The master, an honest man, stopped to recollect. "Bah!" and the under-master came forward and said any number that came into his head. Bonaparte immediately took the mastership from the first and gave it to the second. "*Qu'arrivait il?*" continued Prony; "the rogue who gave the guess answer was soon found cutting down and selling quantities of the trees, and Bonaparte had to take the rangership from him and reinstate the honest hesitator."

Many of her good stories had to be cut short or omitted for lack of time to tell them. "I find always that when I come to the end of my paper I have not told you half the entertaining things I had treasured up for you," she tells her stepmother. As in London, they lived in a constant whirl of gaiety. But Miss Edgeworth never forgot others amid the distinctions paid to herself. She was constantly thinking either what would please those left behind or what kind act she could do for those around her; and if it were nothing more than helping other English visitors to gain a glimpse of French society, she set herself with all ardor to accomplish it:—

Next to the delight of seeing my sisters so justly appreciated and so happy at Paris, my greatest pleasure has been in the power of introducing people to each other, who longed to meet, but could not contrive it before.

Social success did not turn her head:—

Certainly no people can have seen more of the world than we have done in the last three months. By seeing the world I mean seeing varieties of characters and manners, and being behind the scenes of life in many different societies and families. The constant chorus of our moral as we drive home together at night is, "How happy we are to be so fond of each other! How happy we are to be independent of all we see here! How happy that we have our dear home to return to at last!"

Her sisters told on their return how readily Miss Edgeworth would quit the company of the greatest people of the day, to superintend their dress or arrange some pleasure for them. "We often wondered," they said, "what her admirers would say, after all the profound remarks and brilliant witticisms they had listened to, if they heard all her delightful nonsense with us."

The sisters' gay life continued without intermission, only varied now and then by visits to French country houses. Among the most agreeable people they met Miss Edgeworth numbered some Russians and Poles. At the house of the Princess Potemkin she first made wondering acquaintance with, what is now fortunately a matter of course, the more refined mode of serving dinner known as *à la Russe*. She met, too, Prince Rostopchin, the man who burned Moscow by first setting fire to his own house:—

I never saw a more striking Calmuck countenance. From his conversation as well as from his actions I should think him a man of great strength of character. Speaking of the Russians, he compared their civilization to a naked man looking at himself in a gilt-framed mirror, and he told an anecdote that illustrated the perfunctory method of government. The Governor of Siberia lived at Petersburg and never went near his Government. One day the Emperor, in presence of this Governor and Rostopchin, was boasting of his far-sightedness. "Commend me," said Rostopchin, "to M. le Gouverneur, who sees so well from Petersburg to Siberia."

At a breakfast at Camille Jordain's were assembled three of the most distinguished of the party who called themselves *Les Doctrinaires*, and alleged that they were more attached to measures than to men:—

These three doctrinaires were Casimir Perier, Royer Collard and Benjamin Constant, who is, I believe, of a more violent party. I do not like him at all; his countenance, voice, manner and conversation are all disagreeable to me. He is a fair, "whithky" looking man, very near-sighted, with spectacles which seemed to pinch his nose. He pokes out his chin to keep his spectacles on, and yet looks over the top of his spectacles, *squinching* up his eyes, so that you cannot see your way into his mind. Then he speaks through his nose and with a lisp, strangely contrasting with the vehemence of his emphasis. He does not give me any confidence in the sincerity of his patriotism, nor any high idea of his talents, though he seems to have a mighty high idea of them himself. He has been well called *Le Héros des Brochures*. We sat beside one another, and I think felt a mutual antipathy. On the other side of me was Royer Collard, suffering with toothache and swelled face; but notwithstanding the distortion of the swelling, the natural expression of his countenance and the strength and sincerity of his soul made their way, and the frankness of his character and plain superiority of his talents were manifest in five minutes' conversation.

In June Miss Edgeworth and her sisters left Paris for a tour in Switzerland, visiting their friends the Moilliets, who lived at Pregny, near Geneva. Their house, which had formerly belonged to Josephine, commanded a superb view of the lake and of Mont Blanc. It was a surprise to Miss Edgeworth to find how much she was impressed with the beauty of the scenery about her:—

I did not conceive it possible that I should feel so much pleasure from the beauties of nature as I have done since I came to this country. The first moment when I saw Mont Blanc will remain an era in my life—a new idea, a new feeling, standing alone in the mind.

Geneva was at that time enjoying what has been termed its Augustan age. An unusual number of distinguished persons resided there, and it was besides largely resorted to by eminent men and women from all lands, most of whom Miss Edgeworth met at the house of her host. Besides, Monsieur Pictet and Monsieur Dumont, these old, faithful friends, were also domiciled at Geneva, and strove to do the honors of the place. Among temporary residents were such men and women as Dr. and Mrs. Marcet, Arago, De Candolle, the botanist, Freiherr von Stein, Madame Necker de Saussure, and Sismondi. They also met Bonstetten, the poet Gray's youthful friend, then an old man, who spoke with enthusiasm of Madame de Staël.

This mixture of persons from all parts of the world gave a piquancy to the reunions that were held at Geneva. Sometimes the guests met in the evening at a house in town, sometimes at breakfast in the different country villas in all the freshness of the sweet Swiss morning, sometimes by moonlight on lawns sloping down to the lake; when they would sit under trees or stroll about, while tea and ices and the famous varieties of Geneva cakes were handed round. It was at one of these evening assemblies that Miss Edgeworth, while talking to De Candolle in her most brilliant strain, attracted a crowd five deep.

Several short excursions into the lower Alpine regions were made from Geneva by the sisters and their friends; but though Miss Edgeworth enjoyed the beauties of nature beyond her expectations, she yet, as before in her letters, mentions persons and matters of intellectual interest more frequently than scenery. It was a keen gratification to her that M. Dumont spoke well of the now published memoirs. She cared more for this than for the many compliments that were paid to herself, only a few of which she modestly records, and then only because she knows they will please the dear ones at home. At Coppet the party breakfasted with M. de Staël, who showed them all the rooms once inhabited by his mother, which Miss Edgeworth "could not regard as common rooms; they have a classical power over the mind." M. de Staël told her—

That his mother never gave any work to the public in the form in which she had originally composed it. She changed the arrangement and expression of her thoughts with such facility, and was so little attached to her own first views of the subject, that often a work was completely remodeled by her while passing through the press. Her father disliked to see her make any formal preparation for writing when she was young, so that she used to write often on the corner of the chimney-piece or on a pasteboard held in her hand, and always in the room with others, for her father could not bear her to be out of the room, and this habit of writing without preparation she preserved ever afterwards.

M. de Staël told me of a curious interview he had with Bonaparte when he was enraged with his mother, who had published remarks on his government, concluding with "*Eh bien! Vous avez raison aussi. Je conçois qu'un fils doit toujours faire la défense de sa mère, mais enfin, si monsieur veut écrire des libelles, il faut aller en Angleterre. Ou bien s'il cherche la gloire c'est en Angleterre qu'il faut aller. C'est l'Angleterre, ou la France—il n'y a que ces deux pays en Europe—dans le monde.*"

During her absence abroad Miss Edgeworth had revised the manuscript of the latter portion of *Rosamond* and sent it home to press. At the eleventh hour her publisher discovered that there was not enough material to complete two volumes, and urged her to supply more copy without delay. "I was a little provoked," she writes on first hearing the news, "but this feeling lasted but a moment, and my mind fixed on what is to be done. It is by no means necessary for me to be at home or in any particular place to invent or to write." Instantly she set to work, and in the midst of all social attractions and distractions around her she wrote the two additional chapters called *The Bracelet of Memory* and *Blind Kate*.

Late in October the Misses Edgeworth left Switzerland for Paris, visiting Lyons on their way. The town had a special interest for Miss Edgeworth because of her father's early residence there. By the end of October they were once more settled at Paris in a floor to themselves, with a *valet de place* and a *femme de chambre*. Another gay three months followed, seeing old friends and making new ones:—

We have seen Mademoiselle Mars twice, or thrice rather, in the *Mariage de Figaro*, and in the little pieces of *Le jaloux sans amour* and *La jeunesse de Henri Cinq*, and admire her exceedingly. *En petit comité* the other night at the Duchesse d'Escars, a discussion took place between the Duchesse de la Force, Marmont and Pozzo di Borgo on the *bon et mauvais ton* of different expressions; *bonne société* is an expression bourgeoise. You may say *bonne compagnie* or *la haute société*. "*Violà des nuances*," as Madame d'Escars said. Such a wonderful jabbering as these grandees made about these small matters! It puts me in mind of a conversation in the *World* on good company, which we all used to admire.

In December the travellers were back again in London, but several more visits were paid before they returned to Ireland. Thus they halted at Clifton to see Miss Edgeworth's sister Emmeline, who was married there, and stayed at Bowood, Easton Grey, Badminton and various other houses, in all of which they met with a warm welcome. Beloved Aunt Ruxton, too, had to be seen on the way home. It was March before the sisters reached Edgeworthstown, after not quite a year's absence; a year that seemed to Miss

Edgeworth like a delightful dream, full of Alps and glaciers and cascades and Mont Blanc, and "troops of acquaintances in splendid succession and visionary confusion"—a dream of which the sober certainty of happiness remained, assuring her that all that had passed had been no dream, but a reality.

CHAPTER XII.

THE MEMOIRS PUBLISHED.—1821 TO 1825.

THE *Memoirs of Richard Lovell Edgeworth* had been published during Miss Edgeworth's stay on the Continent. After all the anxiety she had felt while preparing the work for the press, she was now able to write to her friends at home:—

You would scarcely believe, my dear friends, the calm of mind and the sort of satisfied resignation I feel as to my father's life. I suppose the two years of doubt and extreme anxiety that I felt exhausted all my power of doubting. I know that I have done my very best, I know that I have done my duty, and I firmly believe that if my dear father could see the whole, he would be satisfied with what I have done.

Still she was sensitive to what those said who had known and loved him; and though Mrs. Ruxton had gone through the manuscript, it was a satisfaction to her to hear that on seeing the work in print she had not altered her views on it. She wrote:—

The irremediable words once past the press, I knew that the happiness of my life was at stake. Even if all the rest of the world had praised it and you had been dissatisfied, how miserable I should have been!

The world was not so lenient in its criticism. It failed to see what right the work had to exist; it acquiesced in what Miss Edgeworth had felt, that she of all persons was the least fitted to be the biographer of the man she so blindly adored.

The first volume is entirely Mr. Edgeworth's own writing, the second is hers; she takes up the narrative on his final removal to Ireland. Although written in his heavy-footed, stilted style, that broke forth now and again into comic pomposity, of the two his is the more entertaining, for he tells many stories that do not concern himself alone. Thus, though he is by no means a graphic writer, we can gather from his pages some notion of the little provincial Mutual Admiration Society that was gathered together at Lichfield under the ægis of Dr. Darwin; of the nature of society in Ireland during his youth; of the state of mechanical science in England. But there is also much that is puerile, some few things that are in bad taste; and the book contains, besides, some really careless blunders with regard to events for which the data were within the reach of all. In Miss Edgeworth's portion it is easily seen that she does not write freely. Even her style, usually more flexible and spontaneous, has caught a reflection from his, while the position in which she stood to the object of her work hindered her from exercising that keen, critical judgment which she possessed, and which would certainly have come to the fore had the subject of her work been a stranger to her. Only while writing about such events as do not immediately deal with her father is she herself. Probably the very anxiety she felt regarding the book was a dim, unformulated consciousness that she had not made it all she desired. The press spoke but coolly. The *Quarterly Review* published a somewhat savage article; indeed, with so much bitterness was it written, that though one is at all times inclined to deprecate the theory of personal enmity, so dear to the wounded vanity of authors, it does suggest the possibility of having been the outcome of malice. But more likely still is it that Mr. Edgeworth's boastful egotism so irritated the writer that he wrote what certainly could not fail to be cruelly wounding to a family who regarded their hero as perfect in all respects. After every allowance has been made for this acrimonious tone (no rare feature in either of the quarterlies in the days of their bumptious youth), the attack certainly contained much that was warranted by circumstances. The writer had not impugned thoughtlessly or ignorantly. He put a sure finger on the contradictions and inaccuracies that occurred in Mr. Edgeworth's narrative, and he gave chapter and verse for his objections. Such criticism, though severe, could not be called wholly unjust. The article, however, raised a perfect storm of indignation among the Edgeworths' Friends. Some called it wicked, others only denounced it as silly. Miss Edgeworth, being in France, was out of the way of seeing the *Quarterly*, and after what she had heard, she simply and wisely resolved never to read it. Indeed, she took the whole matter more philosophically than her friends, and hastened to beg her dearest Aunt Ruxton never to lose another night's sleep or another moment's thought on the *Quarterly Review*. And certainly, whatever the reviewers might say, Miss Edgeworth had the satisfaction before'the year was out of preparing a second edition, and in her seventy-seventh year a third was called for. For this third edition she re-wrote nearly the whole of her portion. With her habitual modesty she assumed that it was her part of the work that had been found long and heavy. Nothing is more touching, more lovable, than the modesty of this woman, so lauded, honored and praised by all her generation that she could not remain ignorant of her fame. But simplicity was the very foundation of her character, and the woman always went before the author.

On her return from France Miss Edgeworth resumed the quiet, dearly-loved routine of home-life. She was always glad to get home again, even now, and to be with the stepmother, sisters and brothers she loved so tenderly. Here is a pretty picture of the daily course of their existence:—

So you like to hear of all our little doings; so I will tell you that, about eight o'clock, Fanny being by that time up and dressed, and at her little table, Harriet comes and reads to me Madame de Sevigné's letters, of which I never tire; and I almost envy Fanny and Harriet the pleasure of reading them for the first time. After breakfast I take my little table into Lucy's room and write there for an hour: she likes to have me in her room, though she only hears the scribble, scribble; she is generally reading at that hour or doing Margaret's delight—algebra. I am doing the sequel to *Frank*. Walking, reading and talking fill the rest of the day. I do not read much; it tires my eyes, and I have not yet finished the *Life of Wesley*. I think it a most curious, entertaining and instructive book. A life of Pitt by the Bishop of Winchester is coming out; he wrote to Murray about it, who asked his friends, "Who is George Winton, who writes to me about publishing Pitt's life?"

Soon after his return from enforced exile Lovell Edgeworth had established a school at Edgeworthstown, after a plan proposed by his father, in which boys of all classes and creeds should be educated together. It succeeded admirably, and was a source of interest and occupation not only to its founder, but to Miss Edgeworth, who always threw herself with ardor into everything that interested those about her.

The lives of women are rarely eventful, and Miss Edgeworth's was perhaps less so than that of most. Her existence moved in the quiet circle of home, and like most women she was much and often occupied with what she happily calls "the necessary business of life, which must be done behind the scenes." The monotony of her existence was only broken by visits to and from friends, and by receiving letters, events in those days of few newspapers, when letters were longer, more detailed than they are now, when they were sent round to a whole circle for perusal, when those who were abroad penned long descriptions of all they saw in what are now beaten tracks familiar to most persons as Piccadilly. The even course of life at Edgeworthstown certainly did not furnish much material for letters except to those interested in the well-being of the numerous members of the household; and Miss Edgeworth's are mostly filled with domestic details of this nature. In August, 1821, she writes:—

What do you think is my employment out of doors, and what it has been this week past? My garden? No such elegant thing; but making a gutter! A sewer and a pathway in the street of Edgeworthstown; and I do declare I am as much interested about it as I ever was in writing anything in my life. We have never here yet found it necessary to have recourse to public contribution for the poor, but it is necessary to give some assistance to the laboring class; and I find that making the said gutter and pathway will employ twenty men for three weeks.

In the late autumn she yielded to the invitations of her many English friends to spend some time among them. She took with her her former travelling companions, for without some of her family Miss Edgeworth felt as if she had left too many pieces of herself behind, and could not enjoy anything thoroughly. Once more the sisters passed some interesting and agreeable months, visiting at the houses of various friends; and during the spring and winter months hiring a house of their own in London, where they entertained and were entertained. They lived in a whirl of town dissipation, knowing six different and totally independent sets: "scientific, literary, political, travelled, artist, and the fine fashionable of various shades." Miss Edgeworth found the different styles of conversation very entertaining, and sent home bright pictures of the various things she saw and heard.

In the hurried life we have led for some weeks past, and among the great variety of illustrious and foolish people we have seen pass in rapid panoramas before us, some remain forever fixed in the memory and some few touch the heart.

At one house Mrs. Somerville was met and thus described:—

Mrs. Somerville—little, slightly made, fair hair, pink color; small, gray, round, intelligent, smiling eyes; very pleasing countenance; remarkably soft voice, strong but well-bred Scotch accent; timid, not disqualifying timid, but naturally modest, yet with a degree of self-possession through it which prevents her being in the least awkward, and gives her all the advantages of her understanding, at the same time that it adds a prepossessing charm to her manner and takes off all dread of her superior scientific learning.

Some days were happily spent visiting Mr. Ricardo, with whose fairness in argument Miss Edgeworth was struck. While her sisters danced, acted charades or played round games, Miss Edgeworth conversed with the elders of the company; but she was ever ready to turn from grave to gay, and often the first to improvise a masquerade or to arrange an impromptu charade. Wherever there was laughter and young people, there she was a favorite and sought-for companion. Her life during these months in England certainly did not lack outward variety, and she was happy for herself, and yet happier because she saw her sisters pleased and beloved. A few extracts from her London letters best reflect her life:—

Yesterday we went, the moment we had swallowed our breakfast, by appointment to Newgate. The private door opened at sight of our tickets, and the great doors and the little doors, and the thick doors and doors of all sorts, were unbolted and unlocked, and on we went through dreary but clean passages, till we came to a room where rows of empty benches fronted us, and a table, on which lay a large Bible. Several ladies and gentlemen entered and took their seats on benches at either side of the table, in silence.

Enter Mrs. Fry in a drab-colored silk cloak, and plain, borderless Quaker cap; a most benevolent countenance—Guido Madonna face—calm, benign.

"I must make an inquiry: Is Maria Edgeworth here, and where?" I went forward: she bade us come and sit beside her. Her first smile as she looked upon me I can never forget. The prisoners came in, and in an orderly manner ranged themselves on the benches. All quite clean faces, hair, caps and hands. On a very low bench in front little children were seated and settled by their mothers. Almost all these women, about thirty, were under sentence of transportation; some few only were there for imprisonment. One who did not appear was under sentence of death—frequently women when sentenced to death became ill and unable to attend Mrs. Fry; the others came regularly and voluntarily.

She opened the Bible and read in the most sweetly solemn, sedate voice I ever heard, slowly and distinctly, without anything in the manner that could distract attention from the matter. Sometimes she paused to explain, which she did with great judgment, addressing the convicts: "*We* have felt; *we* are convinced." They were very attentive, unexpectedly interested, I thought, in all she said, and touched by her manner. There was nothing put on in their countenances, not any appearance of hypocrisy. I studied their countenances carefully, but I could not see any which, without knowing to whom they belonged, I should have decided was bad; yet Mrs. Fry assured me that all of those women had been of the worst sort. She confirmed what we have read and heard, that it was by their love of their children that she first obtained influence over these abandoned women. When she first took notice of one or two of their fine children, the mothers said that if she could but save their children from the misery they had gone through in vice, they would do anything she bid them. And when they saw the change made in their children by her schooling, they begged to attend themselves. I could not have conceived that the love of their children could have remained so strong in hearts in which every other feeling of virtue had so long been dead. The Vicar of Wakefield's sermon in prison is, it seems, founded on a deep and true knowledge of human nature; the spark of good is often smothered, never wholly extinguished. Mrs. Fry often says an extempore prayer, but this day she was quite silent, while she covered her face with her hands for some minutes; the women were perfectly silent with their eyes fixed upon her, and when she said, "You may go," they went away *slowly*. The children sat quite still the whole time; when one leaned, her mother behind sat her upright. Mrs. Fry told us that the dividing the women into classes has been of the greatest advantage, and putting them under the care of monitors. There is some little pecuniary advantage attached to the office of monitor, which makes them emulous to obtain it. We went through the female wards with Mrs. Fry, and saw the women at various works, knitting, rug-making, etc. They have done a great deal of needlework very neatly, and some very ingenious. When I expressed my foolish wonder at this to Mrs. Fry's sister, she replied, "We have to do, recollect, ma'am, not with fools, but with rogues."

*　　*　　*　　*　　*　　*　　*

Far from being disappointed with the sight of what Mrs. Fry has effected, I was delighted. We emerged again from the thick, dark, silent walls of Newgate to the bustling city, and thence to the elegant part of the town; and before we had time to arrange our ideas, and while the mild Quaker face and voice, and wonderful resolution and successful exertion of this admirable woman, were fresh in our minds, morning visitors flowed in and common life again went on.

At Almack's, that exclusive paradise of fashion to which they were admitted, Lord Londonderry came up and talked to Miss Edgeworth about *Castle Rackrent* and Ireland generally. He expressed himself as having been dying with impatience to be introduced to her. She naïvely says:—

It surprised me very much to perceive the rapidity with which a minister's having talked to a person spread through the room. Everybody I met afterwards that night and the next day observed to me that they had seen Lord Londonderry talking to me a great while.

Mrs. Siddons was among the persons whose acquaintance they formed.

She gave us the history of her first acting of Lady Macbeth, and of her resolving, in the sleep scene, to lay down the candlestick, contrary to the precedent of Mrs. Pritchard and all the traditions, before she began to wash her hands and say, "Out, vile spot!" Sheridan knocked violently at her door during the five minutes she had desired to have entirely to herself to compose her spirits before the play began. He burst in and prophesied that she would ruin herself forever if she persevered in this resolution to lay down the candlestick! She persisted, however, in her resolution, succeeded, was applauded, and Sheridan begged her pardon. She described well the awe she felt, and the power of the excitement given to her by the sight of Burke, Fox, Sheridan and Sir Joshua Reynolds in the pit.

Morning, dinner, evening parties, succeeded one another. Miss Edgeworth had not even time to note them. In June (1822) the sisters at last returned home, Miss Edgeworth by no means loth to resume the thread of her domestic affairs. She set to work upon the *Sequel to Harry and Lucy*, which was one among the duty-tasks she deemed it right to do, because her father had wished it to be completed. "I could never be easy writing anything for my own amusement till I had done this, which I know my father wished to have finished."

Portions of Ireland were suffering from famine that summer. The deplorable state of the south in especial aroused all Miss Edgeworth's sympathies. But she feared that as one source of grievance was removed another would spring up.

The minds bent on mischief are unconquered. In fact it is almost the avowed object of the people to drive the remaining resident gentry from the country. I do not think the hatred is between Protestant and Catholic, but between landlord and tenant. I should say, between tenant and landlord. The landlords are the greatest sufferers. Observe, what I have said applies only to the south. The north is in good condition. The neighborhood of Scotland and imported grafted habits of industry have made that part of Ireland almost Scotch. Our tenantry pay comparatively well.

She proceeded to show, however, that they were all at least a year behindhand with their rent, and that Lovell let them pay just when they liked, not insisting upon a rent-day.

In the spring of 1823 Miss Edgeworth and her sisters, Sophy and Harriet, paid some visits in Scotland. At Edinburgh they settled into lodgings near their friends, the Alisons; but the very first evening was spent with Scott, who desired that they should hear some Highland boat-songs at his house. Of this introduction to Scott, and the first evening spent with him, Miss Edgeworth penned a most vivid account.

The next day Scott insisted on showing them the sights of Edinburgh, about whose beauties he was enthusiastic.

His conversation all the time better than anything we could see, full of apropos anecdote, historic, serious or comic, just as occasion called for it, and all with a *bonhommie* and an ease that made us forget it was any trouble even to his lameness to mount flights of eternal stairs.

Indeed, Scott almost took forcible possession of the Misses Edgeworth, so anxious was he to show honor to the author whom he regarded as the most distinguished of contemporary novelists.

How Walter Scott can find time to write all he writes, I cannot conceive. He appears to have nothing to think of but to be amusing, and he never tires, though he is so entertaining. He far surpasses my expectations.

Their delight in each other's society was mutual. Scott wrote to a friend at the time:—

I have very little news to send you. Miss Edgeworth is at present the great lioness of Edinburgh, and a very nice lioness. She is full of fun and spirit; a little slight figure, very active in her motions, very good-humored and full of enthusiasm.

Many of the "Northern Lights" were absent at the time of Miss Edgeworth's visit, but she made the acquaintance of Jeffrey, renewed many old friendships and formed new ties. It was a feature of Miss Edgeworth, as it had been of her father, and it is one that speaks eloquently in favor of their characters, that they never lost a friend or dropped connection with those in whom they had once been interested. Friends once made were friends for life, and were sure of a warm welcome if they came to Ireland, or of a ready answer to any call they might make upon time or heart. Miss Edgeworth's amiable character won for her a far larger circle of friends than her father ever possessed; she had none of those angles in her character which repelled so many from him. Wherever she went she expressed her gratified surprise at the cordiality which people showed towards her, and she met no less of it in Scotland than elsewhere.

After a few weeks spent at Edinburgh William Edgeworth joined his sisters in a tour through the Highlands. Loch Katrine had, of course, special interest to her because of its connection with Scott. She does not think it more beautiful than Killarney: "But where is the lake of our own or any other times that has such delightful power over the imagination by the recollection it raises?"

This Highland tour afforded her great pleasure. "The 'felicity-hunters' have found more felicity than such hunters usually meet with." Unfortunately it ended badly. She caught cold, and was taken ill with a very severe attack of erysipelas that laid her up for ten days in a small Scotch inn. She had been ailing more or less for some months past, and this attack was probably only a climax. As soon as she could move, some friends took her into their house and nursed her tenderly, but she was weak for some time after. But almost before it was true, she tells her stepmother that she is off the invalid list. Scott was anxious to have her at Abbotsford, and promised to nurse her carefully. At the end of July she and her sisters yielded to his friendly entreaties, and spent a fortnight with him in his home. Lockhart speaks of the time of her visit as one of the happiest in Scott's life. Until the Misses Edgeworth arrived the season had been wet. It was a great joy to Sir Walter that with her appearance summer appeared too. On his expressing this, Miss Sophy Edgeworth mentioned the Irish tune, "You've brought the summer with you," and repeated the first line of the words Moore had adapted to it. "How pretty!" said Sir Walter; "Moore's the man for songs. Campbell can write an ode and I can write a ballad, but Moore beats us all at a song."

Miss Edgeworth was charmed with Scott and his home, with the excursions he took with them, with the drives she had with him in his little carriage, during which the flow of his anecdotes, wit and wisdom never ceased. His joyous manner and life of mind, his looks of fond pride in his children, the pleasantness of his easy manners, his keen sense of humor, enchanted her. She also liked Lady Scott, a liking that was returned. Miss Edgeworth considered her

A most kind-hearted, hospitable person, who had much more sense and more knowledge of character and discrimination than many of those who ridiculed her. I know I never can forget her kindness to me when I was ill at Abbotsford. Her last words at parting were: "God bless you! We shall never meet again." At that time it was much more likely that I should have died, I thought, than she.

This was not Miss Edgeworth's first visit to Edinburgh, and Lady Scott expressed her surprise that Sir Walter and she had not met earlier. "Why," said Sir Walter, with one of his queer looks, "you forget, my dear, Miss Edgeworth was not a lion then, and my mane, you know, was not grown at all."

Sir Walter was as sorry to part with his guests as Miss Edgeworth was to go, but she felt that the longer she lingered the more difficult it would be to depart.

After paying some more Scotch visits and a few Irish ones, the Misses Edgeworth returned home in September, and life once more became uneventful. Even to Mrs. Ruxton there was nothing to tell.

It is a long time since I have written to you, always waiting a day longer for somebody's coming or going, or sailing or launching. You ask what I am doing. Nothing but reading and idling, and paving a gutter and yard to Honora's pig-sty and school-house. What have I been reading? The *Siege of Valencia*, by Mrs. Hemans, which is an hour too long, but it contains some of the most beautiful poetry I have read for years.

Sickness, deaths, marriages and births were of frequent occurrence in that large family. Miss Edgeworth's heart was capacious and could answer to all calls made upon it. Whether it was to rejoice with those that rejoiced, or to weep with those that wept, she always responded.

It is the condition, the doom of advancing, advanced age, to see friend after friend go, for so much it detaches one from life; yet it still more makes us value the friends we have left. And continually, at every fresh blow, I really *wonder*, and am thankful, most truly thankful, that I have so many, so much left.

A young sister who had ailed for years, and was obliged to lie flat on a couch, was a constant source of solicitude. What could be done to divert her, to comfort her, or alleviate her sufferings, was always in Miss Edgeworth's mind. Lucy's name often occurs in her letters, and whenever she is absent and there is anything especially amusing to relate, the letter is always addressed to her. In 1824 Miss Edgeworth lost her sister, Mrs. Beddoes. A few months before, Sophy was married to a Captain Fox. She was grieved to lose this sister and the marriage affected her deeply.

Though Miss Edgeworth was now past fifty, she showed neither bodily nor mental signs of advancing years. Indeed, mentally she was as fresh and as young as ever, and her letters reflect the same pleasure in life and all it offers that they evinced throughout. Only on New Year's day, which was also her birthday, does she indulge in any reflections concerning the flight of time. Here is a letter written in 1825:—

A happy new year to you, my dearest aunt, to you to whom I now look, as much as I can to any one now living, for the rays of pleasure that I expect to gild my bright evening of life. As we advance in life, we become more curious, more fastidious in gilding and gilders. We find to our cost that all that glitters is not gold, and your every-day bungling carvers and gilders will not do. Our evening gilders must be more skillful than those who flashed and daubed away in the morning of life, and gilt with any tinsel the weathercock for the morning sun. You may perceive, my dear aunt, by my having got so finely to the weathercock and the rising sun, that I am out of the hands of my dear apothecaries, and playing away again with a superfluity of life. (N. B.—I am surprisingly prudent.) Honora's cough has almost subsided, and Lucy can sit upright the greater part of the day. "God bless the mark!" as Molly Bristow would say, if she heard me; "don't be bragging."

Not many days later, when her stepmother and some friends, "poor souls and full-dress bodies," had gone out to dinner, she penned another long letter to the same correspondent, a letter delightfully fresh in tone and full of her personality:—

In a few days I trust—you know I am a great truster—you will receive a packet franked by Lord Bathurst, containing only a little pocket-book—*Friendship's Offering for 1825*, dizened out. I fear you will think it too fine for your taste, but there is in it, as you will find, the old *Mental Thermometer*, which was once a favorite of yours. You will wonder how it came there. Simply thus: Last autumn came by the coach a parcel containing just such a book as this for last year, and a letter from Mr. Lupton Relfe—a foreigner settled in London—and he prayed in most polite bookseller strain that I would look over my portfolio for some trifle for this book for 1825. I might have looked over "my portfolio" till doomsday, as I have not an unpublished scrap, except *Taken for Granted*. But I recollected the *Mental Thermometer*, and that it had never been *out*, except in the *Irish Farmer's Journal*, not known in England. So I routed in the garret, under pyramids of old newspapers, with my mother's prognostics that I never should find it, and loud prophecies that I should catch my death, which I did not; but dirty and dusty and cobwebby, I came forth, after two hours' groveling, with my object in my hand; cut it out, added a few lines of new end to it, and packed it off to Lupton Relfe, telling him that it was an old thing written when I was sixteen. Weeks elapsed, and I heard no more, when there came a letter exuberant in gratitude, and sending a parcel containing six copies of the new memorandum-book, and a most beautiful twelfth edition of Scott's poetical works, bound in the most elegant manner, and with most beautifully engraved frontispieces and vignettes, and a £5 note. I was quite ashamed—but I have done all I could for him by giving the *Friendship's Offering* to all the fine people I could think of. The set of Scott's works made a nice New Year's gift for Harriet; she had seen this edition at Edinburgh and particularly wished for it. The £5 note I have sent to Harriet Beaufort to be laid out in books for Fanny Stewart. Little did I think the poor old *Thermometer* would give me so much pleasure. Here comes the carriage rolling round. I feel guilty. What will my mother say to me—so long a letter at this time of night? Yours affectionately, in all the haste of guilt, conscience-stricken; that is, found out.

No: all safe, all innocent—because not found out.

FINIS.

By the author of *Moral Tales* and *Practical Education*.

In 1825 Scott paid his long-promised visit to Edgeworthstown. He came in August, bringing with him his daughter, Lockhart and Mr. Crampton, a surgeon friend of the Edgeworths, "who equally gratified both the novelists by breaking the toils of his great practice to witness their meeting on his native soil." Miss Edgeworth writes:—

I am glad that kind Crampton had the reward of this journey; though frequently hid from each other by clouds of dust in their open carriage, they had, as they told us, never ceased talking They like each other as much as two men of so much genius and so much benevolence should, and we rejoice to be the bond of union.

*   *   *   *   *   *   *

Sir Walter delights the heart of every creature who sees, hears and knows him. He is most benignant as well as most entertaining; the noblest and the gentlest of lions, and his face, especially the lower part of it, is excessively like a lion; he and Mr. Crampton and Mr. Jephson were delighted together. The school band after dinner by moonlight playing Scotch tunes, and the boys at leap-frog, delighted Sir Walter. Next day we went to the school for a very short time and saw a little of everything, and a most favorable impression was left. It being Saturday, religious instruction was going on when we went in. Catholics with their priests in one room; Protestants with Mr. Keating in the other. More delightful conversation I have seldom in my life heard than we have been blessed with these three days. What a touch of sorrow must mix with the pleasures of all who have had great losses. Lovell, my mother and I, at twelve o'clock at night, joined in exclaiming, "How delightful! O! that he had lived to see and hear this!"

Of the details of this visit, Lockhart, in his *Life of Scott*, has furnished an account. He draws attention to the curious coincidence that Goldsmith and Maria Edgeworth should both have derived their early love and knowledge of Irish character from the same district, Pallesmore being indeed the property of the Edgeworths.

After a week's stay Sir Walter and his friends departed to visit Killarney; and Miss Edgeworth, her sister Harriet and brother William were easily persuaded to be of the party. The journey was a delightful one to all concerned; and though a few little mishaps occurred, such as the difficulties of finding post-horses to convey so large a party, everything was turned to enjoyment. Sir Walter and Miss Edgeworth shared this faculty of looking on the bright side of the necessary discomforts of a journey, and extracting amusement from every incident—a faculty for want of which so many travellers fail to enjoy themselves. They charmed all with whom they came in contact, down to the very boatman who rowed them on the lake of Killarney, and who, rowing Lord Macaulay twenty years afterwards, told him that the circumstance had made him amends for missing a hanging that day! On Sir Walter Scott's birthday a large gathering of the clans Edgeworth and Scott took place at Dublin. "Sir Walter's health was drunk with more feeling than gaiety," and on that same evening he and Miss Edgeworth parted, never to meet again.

CHAPTER XIII.

1826 TO 1834.

IT was in 1825 that the second part of *Harry and Lucy* was published, completing the labors planned for Miss Edgeworth by her father. The good reception it met with caused her to contemplate writing some more short tales, but she missed the guiding friend that had so long directed her. A story called *Taken for Granted* had long been on the stocks. Though never finished, she was occupied with it for some time, and began to see clearly where her difficulties lay.

Your observations about the difficulties of *Taken for Granted* are excellent; I "take for granted" I shall be able to conquer them. If only one instance were taken, the whole story must turn upon that, and be constructed to bear on one point; and that pointing to the moral would not appear natural. As Sir Walter said to me in reply to my observing, "It is difficult to introduce the moral without displeasing the reader": "The rats won't go into the trap if they smell the hand of the rat-catcher."

The opening of the year 1826 was one of gene"al financial depression. This was, of course, felt yet more acutely in Ireland, where money affairs are never too flourishing. Even the estate of Edgeworthstown, that had as yet safely weathered all storms, was affected, and it was in consequence of this that, at her brother Lovell's desire, Miss Edgeworth once more resumed the rent-receiving and general management, which since her father's death she had abandoned. With consumm'te skill and energy she managed so that her family escaped the flood that swamped so many. For Miss Edgeworth had keen business faculties, though, except in the matter of the estate, they had never been called into play. Her stepmother tells how—

"The great difficulty was paying everybody when rents were not to be had; but Maria, resolutely avoiding the expense and annoyance of employing a solicitor, undertook the whole, borrowing money in small sums, paying off encumbrances, and repaying the borrowed money as the times improved; thus enabling her brother to keep the land which so many proprietors were then obliged to sell. While never distressing the tenants, she at last brought the whole business to a triumphant conclusion."

Yet at no time was Miss Edgeworth absorbed in one thing only; her wide and universal interests could not slumber. Thus, with all the work of a large estate on her hands, she still found time to read extensively. The letters published by Sir Walter Scott under the pseudonym of Sir Malachy Malagrowther had just appeared. They interested her strangely.

Lord Carrington was so kind as to frank to me these extraordinary performances, which shall reach you through Lord Rosse, if you please. It is wonderful that a poet could work up such an enthusiasm about one-pound notes; wonderful that a lawyer should venture to be so violent on the occasion as to talk of brandishing claymores, and passing the fiery cross from hand to hand; and yet there is the Chancellor of the Exchequer answering it from his place in Parliament as a national concern! If Pat had written it, the Attorney-General would, perhaps, have noticed it; but "Up with the shillalah!" in Pat's mouth, and "Out with the claymore!" in Sir Malachy's, are different quite.

A visit from Sir Humphrey Davy during the summer was a great delight. Miss Edgeworth speaks of the range and pitch of his mind with high praise, and relates besides an amusing anecdote that he told:—

Sir Humphrey repeated to us a remarkable criticism of Bonaparte's on Talma's acting: "You don't play Nero well; you gesticulate too much; you speak with too much vehemence. A despot does not need all that; he need only *pronounce. Il sait qu'il se suffit.* And," added Talma, who told this to Sir Humphrey, "Bonaparte, as he said this, folded his arms in his well-known manner, and stood as if his attitude expressed the sentiment."

A little l"ter another sister was taken from the family circle by marriage; this time it was Miss Edgeworth's travelling companion and friend Harriet, who married Mr. Butler, a clergyman. The home party was thinning, and Miss Edgeworth, who liked to have a large number of her loved ones about her, felt this keenly. But happily young nephews and nieces were springing up to take the places of those who were gone, and fill the house with that sunshine of child-life and child-laughter that had seldom been absent from its walls.

She wrote to her brother about a little nephew:—

How you will like that child and make it see "upper air!" How long since those times when you used to show its mother and Harriet upper air! Do you remember how you used to do it to frighten me, and how I used to shut my eyes when you threw them up, and how you used to call me to look? *Ah! Le bon temps!* But we are all very happy now, and it is delightful to hear a child's voice cooing or even crying again in this house.

She was devoted to children, and never happier than when surrounded by them. They in their turn loved the kind little old lady—for she was getting an old lady now—who played with them so merrily, who entered into all their fun, who told them such pretty stories, who plied them with pennies and all manner of good and pretty things. She never lost the power of speaking their language; her letters to children are among some of the most genial she wrote. She was pleased and gratified when the little ones liked her or her stories.

Visits to Mrs. Ruxton at Black Castle, to married brothers and sisters, or to friends, formed more and more frequent interludes in her home-life; but each time she returns, Miss Edgeworth records her excessive happiness to find herself at Edgeworthstown again, with her beloved stepmother and those who still were left.

After one such visit to Mrs. Ruxton, she writes to her:—

After spending four months with you, it is most delightful to me to receive from you such assurances that I have been a pleasure and a comfort to you. I often think of William's most just and characteristic expression, that you have given him a desire to live to advanced age, by showing him how much happiness can be felt and conferred in age, where the affections and intellectual faculties are preserved in all their vivacity. In you there is a peculiar habit of allowing constantly for the *compensating* good qualities of all connected with you, and never unjustly expecting impossible perfections. This, which I have so often admired in you, I have often determined to imitate; and in this my sixtieth year, to commence in a few days, I will, I am resolved, make great progress. "Rosamond at sixty," says Margaret. We are all a very happy party here, and I wish you could see at this moment, sitting opposite to me on a sofa and in an arm-chair, the mother and daughter and grandchild.

The outward course of existence at home was one of quiet routine. Habits of order had been early impressed upon Miss Edgeworth by Mrs. Honora Edgeworth, and though naturally impetuous, she had curbed herself to act with method. It was thanks to these acquired habits that she was able to accomplish daily such a surprising amount of multifarious work. It was her custom to get up at seven, take a cup of coffee, read her letters, and then walk out about three-quarters of an hour before breakfast. So punctual and regular was she that for many years a lady residing in the village used to be roused by her maid with the words, "Miss Edgeworth's walking, ma'am; it's eight o'clock." She generally returned with her hands full of roses or other flowers that she had gathered, and taking her needlework or knitting, would sit down at the family breakfast, a meal that was a special favorite of hers, though she rarely partook of anything. But while the others were eating she delighted to read out to them such extracts from the letters she had received as she thought would please them. She listened, too, while the newspaper was read aloud, although its literary and scientific contents always attracted her more than its political; for in politics, except Irish, she took little interest.

This social meal ended, she would sit down to write, penning letters, attending to business, or inditing stories if any such were in progress. She almost always wrote in the common sitting-room, as she had done during her father's life-time, and for many years on a little desk he had made for her, and on which, shortly before his death, he had inscribed the words:—

On this humble desk were written all the numerous works of my daughter, Maria Edgeworth, in the common sitting-room of my family. In these works, which were chiefly written to please me, she has never attacked the personal character of any human being, or interfered with the opinions of any sect or party, religious or political; while endeavoring to inform and instruct others, she improved and amused her own mind and gratified her heart, which I do believe is better than her head.

R. L. E.

After her father's death she used a writing-desk that had been his, and which accompanied her whenever she went away. At home it was placed on a table he had made, and to which she, inheriting some of his faculty for mechanical inventions, had attached some ingenious contrivances of her own, such as brackets, fire-screens and paper-rests. In summer time this little table was generally rolled into a recess behind the pillars of the library; in winter it stood near the fire. She wrote on folio sheets, which she sewed together in chapters, and her manuscripts were wonderfully neat, clean and free from erasures. At luncheon-time she ceased writing, and since she made this her chief meal in the day, she was obliged, often most unwillingly, to forego her desire to return to her desk. But she knew that to write directly after eating was bad for her, and she submitted instead to doing some needlework. It was while working with her needle, however, that most of her stories were conceived and developed.

Sometimes she would drive out in the afternoon. She was rather nervous about horses, and always sat with her back to them, that she might not see them. When quite at ease on the score of coachman and steeds, she greatly enjoyed a drive in an open carriage, talking and laughing all the time, and amusing her companions with her endless flow of anecdotes and fun. With her habitual indifference to nature she rarely knew and still less cared whither the drive had been directed. Most commonly she wrote again till dinner-time. In her later years she would retire and sleep for an hour after this meal, rejoining the family circle at the tea-table. The evenings were usually spent in reading aloud; sometimes Miss Edgeworth was the reader, sometimes she would work and listen while others read. The enjoyment she felt in literature was imparted to those about her; she would manage to extract something, either knowledge or amusement, out of the dullest book. Her stepmother says that she would often linger after the usual bed-time, to talk over what she had heard, when bright, deep or solid observations would alternate with gay anecdotes apropos of the work or its author. For Miss Edgeworth's best talk was not reserved for abroad, but was rather poured forth at its best when surrounded by those she loved. That her conversation was at all times delightful there is abundant testimony. Mr. Ticknor says of it: "There was a life and spirit about her conversation, she threw herself into it with such *abandon*, she retorted with such brilliant repartee, and, in short, she talked with such extraordinary flow of natural talent, that I don't know whether anything of the kind could be finer."

It is said that even those who came to pay a mere morning call would often remain for hours, loth to terminate the conversation. Nor was her talk by any means uniformly grave; she knew most happily how to blend the grave and gay; she loved to laugh herself and arouse laughter in others, and when she laughed she did so with all the exuberant enjoyment of an Irishwoman. Indeed, there was far more of the light-hearted, merry Irishwoman in Miss Edgeworth than her writings, especially her moral tales, would lead the world to suppose. In her, Irish good qualities were mingled with practical wisdom, judgment and good sense, and produced a combination both rare and charming. She said of herself that she was ugly, remarking that she was the last ugly person left; the rest of the world were no longer anything but plain; but those who knew her did not subscribe to this verdict. She was not, and never had been, good-looking;[10] but a face that beamed such kindliness, reflected such intelligence, could never be really plain. In form she was *petite*; her well-made, almost elegant figure, that remained slight to the last, was enhanced by a scrupulously trim appearance. She was very neat and particular in her dress, and was not only always tidy, but well attired and in accordance with the fashion. She maintained throughout her life that a woman should not be above attending to her dress. Ostentation of any kind was foreign to her nature. When a relative died, leaving her a pair of valuable diamond ear-rings and pearl bracelets, her instant thought was, what good could she do with them? They were sold at once, and with the proceeds she built a village market-house and a room for the magistrate's petty sessions. Her generosity, both in giving money, time and labor for others, was boundless; and her kindnesses were made doubly kind by the thoughtfulness with which they were executed. Thus, for example, many of her tenants and neighbors had relations or friends who had emigrated to the United States. These poor people often found that letters they wrote to America miscarried, a frequent reason being of course insufficient or illegible addresses. To obviate this, Miss Edgeworth caused them to send her all their letters, which she then forwarded once a month. This labor often gave her no small trouble, but she grudged neither this nor the time spent in making up the monthly packet. Her poor neighbors, she deemed, repaid her only too richly by their gratitude. She was certainly one of the few people who practice what they preach; she exemplified in her own person all those judicious plans and rules for helping the needy which she had brought forward in her works. When it is further remembered that Miss Edgeworth retained to the very last, until her eighty-second year, that faculty, which is judged the exclusive gift of youth, of admitting new interests into her life, and that she further made them to run side by side with those she had held of yore, in this mode enriching and widening her mental and emotional horizon, it is little wonder that her old age was one of serene felicity.

The marriage of Fanny Edgeworth, Miss Edgeworth's favorite among all her younger sisters, was a real grief to her for the moment, though, with her usual unselfishness, she upbraided herself for feeling such a "shameful, weak, selfish sorrow at parting with this darling child." A pleasure of a very different kind came to her shortly after in the shape of Sir Walter Scott's introduction to his collected *Waverley Novels*. The sheets, while passing through the press, had been sent to her, and she felt that Scott had, in the most 'elightful and kind manner, said everything that could gratify her "as an author, friend and human creature."

You might well say that I should be "ill to please"—you might have said impossible to please—if what you sent me had not pleased, gratified, delighted me to the top of my bent; saturated me head and heart with the most grateful sense of the kindness of my most admired friend, and with the unspeakable gratification of such a testimony of his esteem and affection. I know full well, most sincerely I feel, that he over-values infinitely what I have written; but of this I am proud, because it proves to me that private friendship of his which I value above all, even his public praise....

Believe me, my dear sir, I feel it all; and if I could, as you say, flatter myself that Sir Walter Scott was in any degree influenced to write and publish this novel from seeing my sketches of Irish character, I should indeed triumph in the thought of having been the proximate cause of such happiness to millions.

Among the many advanced movements that Mr. Edgeworth had advocated was the cause of Catholic emancipation. In such public measures as her father had felt an interest, Miss Edgeworth felt one too; and it was a great joy to her that not only she, but her father's sister, had lived to see this measure carried. It is amusing to learn that it was a grievance of O'Connell's against Miss Edgeworth that she never directly espoused this cause by means of her pen. This was, in real fact, a compliment, as showing what a power her writings had become.

In the summer, the "reaper whose name is Death" reappeared amidst that united family, carrying off this time the able engineer, William Edgeworth, who also succumbed to the fatal family malady. It was a shock and a grief to his devoted sister, who sorrowed the more when she saw her juniors go before her, and the grief told on her own health. She was ailing until autumn, often confined to the sofa and forbidden her pen, though, happily for her, neither her needle nor her books. Her idle fancy began once more to weave romances, and she planned the story of *Helen* and made some notes for it. Contrary to her previous custom, she did not draw up a complete sketch, as she had done while writing under her father's guidance. She jotted down the rough outlines, and trusted to spontaneous promptings to fill in the details. But she was not even certain at all whether she should attempt to write it; and although encouraged by the success of *Harry and Lucy*, she was nervous about grappling with higher work, deprived of the guide who had been her life-long stay.

For years she had rejected all suggestions to turn her attention once more to novel-writing, and but for the encouragement of her sister Harriet (Mrs. Butler), *Helen* would probably never have seen the light. It was first seriously thought of in 1830, but proceeded slowly. Life brought more interruptions to her than it had done in youth—family events, visits of kindness and pleasure, absorbed much time. Then, too, she was greatly engrossed by her agency business, to which all else was made to defer. She was punctual, we are told, not only to the day, but to the hour, of her payments; and her exertions to have the rents paid and the money ready for these payments were unvarying. She herself looked after the repairs, the letting of the village houses, the drains, gutters and pathways, the employment of the poor,—in short, all the hundred and one duties that devolve upon the steward of landed property. It was considered by her family that all this exertion was in no wise too much for her; that, on the contrary, it was good for her health, inducing her to walk out and take more exercise than she would have done without an object in view. Even the very drudgery of accounts and letters of business, says her stepmother, "though at times almost too much for her bodily strength, invigorated her mind; and she went from the rent-book to her little desk and the manuscript of *Helen* with renewed vigor. She never wrote fiction with more life and spirit than when she had been for some time completely occupied with the hard realities of life."

Nevertheless, *Helen* progressed slowly, and was several times in danger of being thrust aside. She wrote to her sister:—

My dear Harriet, can you conceive yourself to be an old lamp at the point of extinction, and dreading the smell you would make at going out, and the execrations which in your dying flickerings you might hear? And then you can conceive the sudden starting up again of the flame when fresh oil is poured into the lamp. And can you conceive what that poor lamp would feel returning to light and life? So felt I when I had read your letter on reading what I sent to you of *Helen*. You have given me new life and spirit to go on with her. I would have gone on from principle, and the desire to do what my father advised—to finish whatever I began; but now I feel all the difference between working for a dead or a live horse.

To the day of her death Miss Edgeworth never became the prudent, staid, self-contained person we should imagine her from her books, did we possess them only as guides to her character. *Rosamond* remained as generously impulsive as ever. On one occasion she writes to Mrs. Ruxton:—

It is very happy for your little niece that you have so much the habit of expressing to your kind feelings. I really think that if my thoughts and feelings were shut up completely within me, I should burst in a week, like a steam engine without a snifting-clack, now called by the grander name of a safety-valve. You want to know what I am doing and thinking of: of ditches, drains and sewers, of dragging quicks from one hedge and sticking them down into another, at the imminent peril of their green lives; of two houses to let, one tenant promised from the Isle of Man, another from the Irish Survey; of two bullfinches, each in his cage on the table—one who would sing if he could, and the other who could sing, I am told, if he would. Then I am thinking for three hours a day of *Helen*, to what purpose I dare not say.

Before the year 1830 was ended Miss Edgeworth had lost this aunt, whom she had loved so long and fondly. It was the severing of a life-long friendship, the heaviest blow that had befallen her since her father's death. She was in London when the event took place, and it was some comfort to her to find herself so kindly welcomed by those whom she had liked best in years gone by. She says sadly:—

It is always gratifying to find old friends the same after long absence, but it has been particularly so to me now, when not only the leaves of the pleasures of life fall naturally in its winter, but when the great branches on whom happiness depended are gone.

During this visit she kept out of all large parties, but renewed many old ties. One of the things she enjoyed most was a children's party at Mrs. Lockhart's. She was in her element among the young ones. "If Mrs. Lockhart had invented forever she could not have found what would please me more." This London visit extended over some months:—

Old as I am, and imaginative as I am thought to be, I have really always found that the pleasures I have expected would be great, have actually been greater in the enjoyment than in the anticipation. This is written in my sixty-fourth year. The pleasure of being with Fanny has been far, far greater than I had expected. The pleasures here altogether, including the kindness of old friends and the civilities of acquaintances, are still more enhanced than I had calculated upon by the home and the quiet library and easy-chair morning retreat I enjoy.

On her return to Edgeworthstown she wrote:—

My last visit to universal London confirms to my own feelings your eulogium. I never was so happy there in my life, because I had, besides all the external pleasures, the solid satisfaction of a home there, and domestic pleasures, without which I should soon grow aweary of the world, and wish the business of the town were done. It is most gratifying to me, at such a distance, to hear and to believe that such kind and cultivated friends as you miss my company and wish for my future return. I should be very sorry if I were told this minute that I was never to see London again, and yet I am wondrous contented and happy at home.

It is a curious circumstance, but a fact of frequent observation, that large families are often more united than small ones. The Edgeworths were a case in point. They had that devoted affection, that blind belief in one another, that often distinguishes a clan. They preferred each other's society to that of strangers; they regarded themselves as beings apart; what one did, the others approved; harmony and good will reigned supreme. With so many different families living under one roof, it was a rare and curious fusion, this home party, of which one of the brothers said that "each star is worthy of separate observation for its serenity, brilliancy or magnitude; but it is as a constellation they claim most regard, linked together by strong attachment and moving in harmony through their useful course."

It was as a star of the first magnitude in this constellation that Miss Edgeworth loved to move and have her being, and she chose to be set there rather than shine in brilliancy alone. Miss Edgeworth, the woman, must always be thought of in connection with her home and home attachments. To love, shrouded in the quiet obscurity of domestic life, was the secret of existence to this simple-minded nature.

That *Helen* was liked by the home circle was a real pleasure to its author. She was anxious for criticism and took all she received in good part. "I am a creature," she once said, "that can take advice, can be the better for it, and am never offended by it." The family approval given, the manuscript was despatched to London with more confidence than she had ever expected to feel again in a literary work. Lockhart managed the business arrangements, for to this she did not feel equal, and when asked if the book should be in two or three volumes, replied:—

I have satisfied my own conscience, which is my point, as I know that far from having stretched a single page, or a single sentence, to *make out* a third volume, I have cut as much as ever I could—cut it to the quick; and now it matters not whether it be printed in three or in two volumes. If tiresome to the ear in three, it would be equally so in two, and would look worse to the eye.

The reason why her new story was not an Irish one she gives in a letter to a brother in India:—

I should tell you beforehand that there is no humor in it and no Irish character. It is impossible to draw Ireland as she now is in a book of fiction—realities are too strong, party passions too violent to bear to see, or care to look at their faces in the looking-glass. The people would only break the glass and curse the fool who held the mirror up to nature—distorted nature, in a fever. We are in too perilous a case to laugh: humor would be out of season, worse than bad taste. Whenever the danger is passed, as the man in the sonnet says, "We may look back on the hardest part and laugh." Then I shall be ready to join in the laugh. Sir Walter Scott once said to me, "Do explain to the public why Pat, who gets forward so well in other countries, is so miserable in his own." A very difficult question; I fear above my power. But I shall think of it continually, and listen, and look, and read.

Things were once more in a bad way in that unhappy country, and Miss Edgeworth saw great distress all around her. A letter written at that time might almost be written to-day:—

I fear we have much to go through in this country before we come to quiet, settled life, and a ready obedience to the laws. There is literally no rein of law at this moment to hold the Irish; and through the whole country there is what I cannot justly call a spirit of *reform*, but a spirit of *revolution*, under the name of reform; a restless desire to overthrow what *is*, and a hope—more than a hope—an expectation of gaining liberty or wealth, or both, in the struggle; and if they do gain either, they will lose both again and be worse off than ever—they will afterwards quarrel amongst themselves, destroy one another, and be again enslaved with heavier chains. I am and have been all my life a sincere friend to moderate measures, as long as reason can be heard; but there comes a time, at the actual commencement of uproar, when reason cannot be heard, and when the ultimate law of force must be resorted to, to prevent greater evils. *That time was lost in the beginning of the French Revolution*—I hope it may not be lost in Ireland. It is scarcely possible that this country can now be tranquilized without military force to reestablish law; the people *must* be made to obey the laws or they cannot be ruled after any concessions. Nor would the mob be able to rule if they got all they desire; they would only tear each other to pieces, and die *drunk* or famish *sober*. The misfortune of this country has been that England has always yielded to *clamor* what should have been granted to justice.

As Miss Edgeworth advanced in life she often spoke of "my poor Ireland," showing that hopelessness with regard to the problem had dawned on her. She was a patriot, but belonged to no party; and was blind neither to the nation's wrongs, follies nor crimes. She grew more and more to advocate the *laissez-faire* system. She contended that her observations, which extended over so long a period of time, had shown her steady progression in Ireland, and she believed that the land would ultimately do well if people would only not force their political nostrums upon it. What she did demand from England was equality of legislation, but no more; and this accorded, she believed Ireland would rise from her state of degradation, though of necessity the rise would be slow, since the length of time of recovery must be in proportion to the length and force of the infliction. Mrs. Hall very rightly remarked that Miss Edgeworth's affection for Ireland was "philosophic." Yet another change Miss Edgeworth observed in the Irish, and one that made them less useful to her for literary purposes:—

The modern peasantry imagine they have a part to play in the organization of their country; their heads are fuller of politics than fun; in fact, they have been drilled into thinking about what they cannot understand, and so have become reserved and suspicious—that is, to what they used to be.

After *Helen* had passed through the press, Miss Edgeworth accompanied her friends Sir Culling and Lady Smith in a trip through Connemara. Of the adventures they had on this journey—real Irish adventures, with innumerable sloughs to traverse, with roads that imperilled life, with inns whose dirt and discomfort passed belief, with roadside hospitality from kindly but eccentric gentlefolks—Miss Edgeworth wrote a letter some forty pages long to a brother in India. For fun and graphic vivacity it is not surpassed by the best of her printed Irish scenes. After her return "rents and odious accounts" kept her mind from running too much upon *Helen*, about which she was more anxious than about any book she had ever sent into the world. It soon proved as great a success as her earlier works, and a second edition was demanded after a few weeks. Her own feelings about the matter are expressed in a letter she wrote to Mr. Bannatyne, who had congratulated her on its public reception:—

MY DEAR MR. BANNATYNE:

I thank you with all my heart for the "nervousness" you felt about my venturing again before the public, and it is a *heart*-felt as well as a *head*-felt satisfaction to me that you do not think I have lowered what my father took such pains to raise for me. You cannot conceive how much afraid I was myself to venture what had not his corrections and his sanction. For many, many years that feeling deterred me from any attempt in this line. Of what consequence, then, to my happiness it is to be assured, by friends on whose sincerity and judgment I can depend, that I have not done what I ought to repent or to be ashamed of.

Concerning *Helen* contemporary public opinion was much divided; some regarded it as a falling-off in power, others as an advance, but all agreed that there was a change. The change is one of tone and feeling, induced in part, no doubt, by the fact that it was the emanation of her own brain only; in part that years had caused Miss Edgeworth, as it causes all of us, to regard life from a different standpoint. Experience had taught her to

Gentler scan her brother man

than she did in earlier life. *Helen* is so much superior in ease, nature and poetry, that it makes us deplore that Miss Edgeworth's talents had not been allowed unchecked sway. Not only is the fable more skillfully framed, but the whole shows greater passion and finer insight into the more subtle moods of humanity. Too often when men and women go on writing far into their latter years we are apt to wish that, like Prospero, they had buried their wand before it had lost its power. This is not the case with Miss Edgeworth. *Helen*, her last novel, which appeared after so long a silence, is in some respects the most charming of her tales—a fact doubtless due in some measure to the time that had elapsed since the cessation of her father's active influence. The old brilliancy, the quick humor, the strong sense of justice and truth which is the moral backbone of her work, are there as before; but through the whole tale there breathes a new spirit of wider tenderness for weak, struggling human nature, and a gentleness towards its foibles, which her earlier writings lacked. Years had taught her a wider toleration, had shown her, too, how large a part quick, unreasoning instincts and impulses play in the lives of men and women, even of those whose constant struggle it is to subdue act and thought to the rule of duty. *Helen* is more of a romance than any of its predecessors, perhaps because the chief interest of the tale is concentrated in the heroine, who is the central figure round which the other persons of the story revolve, while in Miss Edgeworth's earlier novels the subsidiary characters are the most interesting and amusing. We wish Belinda well, but she does not move our feelings as does Lady Delacour, and Sir Philip Baddeley is infinitely more diverting than Clarence Harvey is fascinating. And it is the same in all the others, while the centre of *Helen* is the girl herself. Yet the other characters are no less admirably drawn, with the old delicacy and firmness of touch, the occasional quaint gleams of humor. In its way Miss Edgeworth never limned a finer portrait than that of Lady Davenant, the large-brained, large-hearted woman of the world, endowed with strong principle, keen sense and real vigor of character, mingled with prejudice, impulsive likes and dislikes, an imperfect adherence in practice to her own theories of right and wrong, and a stern power of self-judgment. There is nothing exaggerated in this admirable and vigorous piece of work. We comprehend Cecilia's nervous fear of the mother whose unswerving truth cows her, while it attracts the answering truth of nature of her truer and stronger friend. Equally good is the character of Lady Cecilia, through whose duplicity and cowardice arise all Helen's troubles; her husband, General Clarendon, who held

All fraud and cunning in disdain,

A friend to truth, in speech and action plain;

the malicious Lady Beatrice and her silly, pretty sister; while Horace Churchill, the man about town, who is more modern in tone than Miss Edgeworth's earlier portraits of the same class, loses nothing by comparison with them. Despite his restless egotism, his spitefulness, his generally unpleasant character, he is a gentleman in all outside seeming, the old-fashioned, perfect tone of high breeding marks him, and he is even capable of a certain generosity that seems more an inherited instinct than a part of his individual nature. Esther, the general's sister, is one of the quaintest and most delightful characters in the book, drawn with kindliness and humor— a girl with the power of a noble woman hidden under the crust of a gruff and abrupt exterior, which springs half from shyness, half from a defiant love of truth and hatred of conventional chains. The purpose of *Helen* is to show how much the sufferings and dissensions of social life arise from the prevailing digressions from truth, often due in the first instance to small society politenesses. Its key-note lies in the ejaculation of Miss Clarendon: "I wish that word *fib* was out of the English language, and *white lie* drummed out after it. Things by their right names, and we should all do much better. Truth must be told, whether agreeable or not." Most perfectly and naturally is the imbroglio brought to pass, the entanglement caused by the love-letters, the way in which every fresh deceit on the part of Cecilia, meant to be harmless, tells in her husband's mind against the friend behind whom she is basely hiding her own fault. With Cecilia, whose failings were of the kind with which Miss Edgeworth had least mercy, she is singularly gentle. For once she lets us pity the offender while we condemn the crime. Life had probably taught her that consequences are so surely unpitying that she no longer felt the need to insist on this, as she had done in former years, when she would probably have sketched for us the whole course of Cecilia's punishment, whose nature she now only indicates. Helen is a charming heroine; no wax doll of impossible perfection, but a very woman, wayward and weak sometimes, but true, high-spirited, impulsively generous, staunch in her friendship and her love, with deep and passionate feelings controlled, not crushed, by duty.

Another marked change is shown in the manner in which Helen and Granville Beauclerc fall in love. Miss Edgeworth had always protested against the doctrine that love is a mere matter of personal beauty; she showed how it may enslave for a moment, but that a preference resting on so precarious a foundation was but a paltry tribute to her sex. Love, she rightly preached, must be founded on higher motives; but her heroes and heroines were too apt to fall in love in an edifying and instructive manner; they know too well why they succumbed to the tender passion. Until now she had almost denied the existence of romantic love, agreeing, it would seem, with her own Mrs.

Broadhurst: "Ask half the men you are acquainted with why they are married, and their answer, if they speak the truth, will be: 'Because I met Miss Such-a-one at such a place, and we were continually together.'" "'Propinquity, propinquity,' as my father used to say—and he was married five times, and twice to heiresses." That amiable and respectable Bluebeard, Miss Edgeworth's father, had hitherto held final sway over her characters. Was it the remov'l of this influence that allowed Helen and Granville to fall in love in a more'rational manner? Helen does not now wait to see whether Beauclerc has every virtue under the sun before she ventures to love him; indeed, she sees his foibles clearly, and it is just when she believes that he has shown a lack of honor and sincerity that in her burst of grief she discovers that she loves him; loves him whatever he is, whatever he does. As for Granville, he falls in love in a thorough-going, earnest manner, which increases our feeling of his reality. It has been objected to Miss Edgeworth's love-making that it is stiff as compared with that of the present day. It certainly presents a contrast to that of the Broughton school; but the loves of Helen and Granville, as told by her in so real and human a manner, reveal their feelings to be none the less tender that they are not hysterical, or any the less deep for their power of modesty, reverence and reserve.

Helen was suggested by Crabbe's tale, *The Confidant*, but that feeling which is sinfully gratified and severely punished in Crabbe's story becomes refined and reformed in Miss Edgeworth's crucible. It is, however, interesting to compare her romance with the rapid sketch of the stern original. Another new feature in *Helen* is a tendency to describe natural objects. Until now there had never been in Miss Edgeworth's writings a description of scenery or a sign of delight in it. She had, as we know, a contempt for the mere pleasures of the senses, and so little appreciation of the beautiful that she once condemns a character who buys something to gratify the eye, not recognizing that the eye, as well as the body and mind, must be fed. Yet in *Helen*, to our surprise, we encounter some lovingly detailed scenic bits; we even find her citing Wordsworth. It is clear she had not remained wholly untouched by the new influences surging around her. Another feature of *Helen* is the lack of a didactic tone. Speaking of Scott's novels, she remarks that his morality is not in purple patches, ostentatiously obtrusive, but woven in through the very texture of the stuff. She knew that her faults lay in the opposite direction, and it is evident she had striven to avoid them. A writer who can learn from criticism and experience, who can adopt a new method of writing when past the age of sixty, is a remarkable writer indeed.

The fears that Miss Edgeworth had felt concerning *Helen* were truly uncalled for, but the eagerness with which she listened to criticisms upon it showed how little confident she felt of it herself. To her friend Dr. Holland she wrote after its appearance:—

DEAR SIR:

I am very glad that you have been pleased with *Helen*—far above my expectations! And I thank you for that warmth of kindness with which you enter into all the details of the characters and plan of the story. Nothing but regard for the author could have made you give so much importance to my tale. It has always been my fault to let the moral end I had in view appear too soon and too clearly, and I am not surprised that my old fault, notwithstanding some pains which I certainly *thought* I took to correct it, should still abide by me. As to Lady Davenant's loving Helen better than she did her daughter—I can't help it, nor could she. It is her fault, not mine, and I can only say it was very natural that, after having begun by mistake and neglect in her early education, she should feel afterwards disinclined to one who was a constant object of self-reproach to her. Lady Davenant is not represented as a perfect character. All, then, that I have to answer for is, whether her faults are natural to the character I drew, and tend in their representation to the moral I would *enforce* or *insinuate*.

Oh, thank you for telling me of my blunder in making the dean die of *apoplexy* with his eyes fixed on Helen. Absurd! How shall I kill him in the next edition, if ever I am allowed an opportunity? Would palsy do? May there not be a partial power of *will* surviving a stroke of palsy, which would permit the poor old man to die with his eyes directed to his niece? Please to answer this question; and if palsy will not do my business, please to suggest something that will, and with as little alteration of the text as maybe. Not because I am unwilling to take the trouble of correcting, but that I don't think it worth while to make alterations, even emendations, of great length. Better make a new one, according to Pope's hackney coachman's principle. (The punctuation shall be mended.)

CHAPTER XIV.

LAST YEARS.

MORE and more Miss Edgeworth's life revolved round home and friends. "In this world, in which I have lived nearly three-quarters of a century, I have found nothing one-quarter so well worth living for as old friends," she said. In her person old age was seen in its most attractive form. Her lively interests remained undimmed. At seventy she even set herself to learn a new language, Spanish, while her impulsiveness never became extinct, though she playfully hoped that, provided she lived so long, she might perhaps at eighty arrive at years of discretion. It was in 1835 that Mr. Ticknor, the American historian of Spanish literature, visited Edgeworthstown. He has recorded in his journal a pleasing and vivid picture of his visit. He describes Miss Edgeworth as small, short and spare, with frank and kind manners, always looking straight into the face of those she spoke to with a pair of mild, deep gray eyes. Her kindness and vivacity instantly put her visitors at ease. Mr. Ticknor was also impressed with the harmony that existed in a family composed of the most heterogeneous relationships. What struck him about Miss Edgeworth herself was her uncommon quickness of perception, her fertility of allusion, and the great resources of fact which a remarkable memory supplied to her. He likens her conversation to that of her own Lady Davenant. Mr. Ticknor observed that though she would talk freely about herself and her works, she never introduced the subject, and never seemed glad to continue it. Indeed, though he watched carefully for it, he could not detect either any of the mystification or the vanity of authorship. He was struck with her good nature and desire to defend everybody, even Lady Morgan, as far as she could, though never so far as to be unreasonable.

"In her intercourse with her family she was quite delightful, referring constantly to Mrs. Edgeworth, who seems to be the authority in all matters of fact, and most kindly repeating jokes to her infirm aunt, Mrs. Sneyd, who cannot hear them, and who seems to have for her the most unbounded affection and admiration."

The dispersion of so many"members of her family imposed much letter-writing on Miss Edgeworth, for all turned to her graphic pen for news of the dear old home. And, as before when she was away, those she left behind had to share in her pleasures, or they would be but sorry pleasures to her. Death, as well as marriages, had thinned the family ranks. Tenacious and warm in her affections as she was, Miss Edgeworth never took a morbid view concerning those who were gone. Everything morbid was foreign to her nature.

There is something mournful, yet pleasingly painful, in the sense of the ideal presence of the long-loved dead. Those images people and fill the mind with unselfish thoughts, and with the salutary feeling of responsibility and constant desire to be and to act in this world as the superior friend would have wished and approved.

And there were so many still left to love, young and old. "Who would not like to live to be old if they could be so happy in friends as I am?" The enthusiastic affection in her peculiar family relations, which she kept unimpaired, cannot be better shown than by quoting one of the countless letters she wrote concerning those dear to her:—

EDGEWORTHSTOWN, NOV. 1, 1838.

MY DEAR MR. AND MRS. TICKNOR:

I know so well your kind feelings towards all this family, that I am sure you will be pleased with the intelligence which I am going to communicate to you.

My sister Honora is going to be happily married to a person every way suited to her (and that is saying a great deal), as you who most kindly and justly appreciated her will readily join with me in thinking. The gentleman's name, Captain Beaufort, R. N., perhaps you may be acquainted with, as he is in a public situation, and not unknown to literary and scientific fame. He is a naval officer. (I hope you like this officer's name?) He made some years ago a survey of the coast of Caramania, and wrote a small volume on that survey, which has obtained for him a good reputation. He has been for some years Hydrographer Royal.... In one word, he is a person publicly esteemed; and privately he is beloved and esteemed by all who know him best. He is and has been well known to us ever since the present Mrs. Edgeworth's marriage with my father. Captain Beaufort is Mrs. Edgeworth's youngest brother. As Mrs. E. is Honora's *step*mother, you see that he is no relation whatever to Honora. But the nearness of the connection has given us all the best means of knowing him thoroughly. He was my dear father's most beloved pupil and friend; by pupil I only mean that his being so much younger made him look up to my father with reverence, and learn from him in science and literature with delight. Thus has he been long connected with all I love. He has been a widower two years. He has three sons and four daughters.... The youngest daughter, Emily, is a delightful child. Captain Beaufort lives in London, 11 Gloucester place; has a very comfortable house, and sufficient fortune for all their moderate wishes. Honora's fortune, which is ample, will give them affluence.

My dear Mrs. Ticknor, I know you particularly liked Honora, and that you will be interested in hearing all these particulars, though it seems impertinent to detail them across the Atlantic to one who will, I fear, never see any one of the persons I have mentioned. Yet affections such as yours keep warm very long and at a great distance.

I feel that I have got into a snug little corner in both your hearts, and that you will excuse a great deal from me; therefore I go on without scruple drawing upon your sympathy, and you will not protest my draft.

You saw how devoted Honora was to her aunt, Mrs. Mary Sneyd, whom you liked so much; and you will easily imagine what a struggle there has been in Honora's mind before she could consent to a marriage with even such a man as Captain Beaufort, when it must separate her from her aunt. Captain Beaufort himself felt this so much that he never would have pressed it. He once thought that she might be prevailed upon to accompany them to London and to live with them. But Mrs. Mary Sneyd could not bear to leave Mrs. Edgeworth, and this place which she has made her heart's home. She decided Captain Beaufort and her niece to make her happy by completing their union, and letting her feel that she did not prevent the felicity of the two persons she loves best now in the world. She remains with us.

The marriage is to take place next Tuesday or Thursday, and my Aunt Mary will go to the church with her niece and give her away. I must tell you a little characteristic trait of this aunt, the least selfish of all human beings. She has been practicing getting up early in the morning, which she has not done for two years—has never got up for breakfast. But she has trained herself to rising at the hour at which she must rise on the wedding-day, and has walked up and down her own room the distance she must walk up and down the aisle of the church, to insure her being accustomed to the exertion and able to accomplish it easily. This she did for a long time without our knowing it, till Honora found it out. Mrs. Mary Sneyd is quite well and in excellent spirits.

A younger sister of mine, Lucy, of whom you have heard us speak as an invalid, who was at Clifton with that dear Sophy whom we have lost, is now recovered, and has returned home to take Honora's place with her Aunt Mary; and Aunt Mary likes to have her, and Lucy feels this a great motive to her to overcome a number of nervous feelings, which formed part of her illness. A regular course of occupations and duties, and feeling herself essential to the happiness and the holding together of a family she so loves, will be the best strengthening medicine for her. She arrived at home last night. My sister Fanny and her husband, Lestock Wilson, are with us. My sister has much improved in health; she is now able to walk without pain, and bore her long journey and voyage here wonderfully. I have always regretted, and always shall regret, that this sister Fanny of mine had not the pleasure of becoming acquainted with you. You really must revisit England.

My sister Harriet Butler, and Mr. Butler, and the three little dear Foxes, are all around me at this instant. Barry Fox, their father, will be with us in a few days, and Captain Beaufort returns from London on Monday. You see what a large and happy family we are!!!

Do I not give you some proof, my dear Mr. and Mrs. Ticknor, of my affection in writing to you at this moment? And if I write without much sense or connection you will not be surprised.

My head is really upside down, and my feelings so divided between joy and sorrow—joy for Honora's happiness, but sorrow for the parting that must be!

It will all settle down under the hand of strong necessity and of lenient time. My sisters Fanny and Harriet will stay with us some weeks after the marriage; this will be a great comfort.

Mr. Butler will perform the happy, awful ceremony. How people who do not love can ever dare to marry, to approach the altar to pronounce that solemn vow, I cannot conceive.

My thoughts are so engrossed by this subject that I absolutely cannot tell you of anything else. You must tell me of everything that interests you, else I shall not forgive myself for my egotism.

I am most sincerely and affectionately, my dear Mrs. Ticknor, with affectionate remembrances to your engaging daughter, not forgetting your little darling,

Yours most sincerely,

MARIA EDGEWORTH.

Mention Lockhart's *Memoirs of Scott*, of which my head and heart were full before this present all-engrossing subject overcame me.

I shall be quite rational again, I am sure, by the time your answer reaches me, so pray do not treat me as quite a hopeless person to write rationally to.

Mrs. Edgeworth desires me to send you her very affectionate remembrances.

I believe, I am almost sure, that I wrote to you, my dear Mr. Ticknor, some months ago while you were on the Continent, to thank you for the present you sent me, through Mr. Norton's means, of an American edition of my works. I thought it beautifully printed and bound, and the engravings excellent, particularly that for *Helen*, and the vignette for *Helen*, which we have not in the English edition. I have another American copy of this edition, and I have left yours for life with my brother Francis and my Spanish sister Rosa, who live in a little cottage near Windsor, and have not money to indulge themselves in the luxury of books. I hope you will not be angry with me for so doing; no, I think you will be glad that I made your present give me the greatest possible sum of pleasure. Take into account the pride I felt in saying, *Mr. Ticknor sent me these books.*

I am ashamed to see that I have come so far in a second sheet, and in spite of all the wonderings at what can Maria *be about?*

Sense in my next.

In answer to a letter from Mr. Ticknor, describing to her his library, in which the only picture was one of Sir Walter Scott, Miss Edgeworth wrote a reply, of which a portion has been published, but which contains besides an able parallel, or rather contrast, between Washington and Napoleon, worthy of preservation for its own sake, and as a testimony to her unimpaired powers:—

TRIM, NOV. 19TH, 1840.

"Who talks of '*Boston*' in a voice so sweet?" Who wishes to see me there? And to show me their home, their family, their country? I have been there— at Boston! "Yes, and in Mr. and Mrs. Ticknor's happy, beautiful home." I have been up "the slope of the Boston hillside," have seen "the fifty acres of public park" in all its verdure, with "its rich and venerable trees," its graveled promenade surrounding it, with those noble rows of venerable elms on either side. I have gone up the hillside and the steps profusely decked with luxuriant creepers; I have walked into Mr. and Mrs. Ticknor's house, as I was desired— have seen the three rooms opening into one another, have sat in the library, too, and thought—and thought it all charming. Looking into the country, as you know the windows all do, I saw down through "the vista of trees" to the quiet bay and the "beautiful" hills beyond, and I "watched the glories of the setting sun" lighting up country and town, "trees, turf and water!"—an Italian sun not more gorgeously attended than this "New England luminary" setting or rising. I met Sir Walter Scott in Mr. Ticknor's library with all his benign, calm expression of countenance, his eye of genius and his mouth of humor—such as he was before the life of life was gone, such as genius loved to see him, such as American genius has *given* him to American friendship, immortalized in person as in mind. His very self I see feeling, thinking and about to speak—and to a friend to whom he loved to speak; and well placed and to his liking he seems in this congenial library, presiding and sympathizing. But my dear madam, ten thousand books, "about ten thousand books," do you say this library contains? My dear Mrs. Ticknor! Then I am afraid you must have double rows—and that is a plague. But you may ask why do I conceive you have double rows? Because I cannot conceive how else the book-cases could hold the ten thousand. Your library is 34 by 22, you say. But to be sure you have not given me the height, and that height may make out room enough. Pray have it measured for me, that I may drive this odious notion of *double rows* out of my head—"and what a head," you may say, "that must be that could calculate in such a place and at such a time!" It was no" my poor head, I assure you, my dear Mrs. Ticknor, but Captain Beaufort's ultra-accurate head. I gave him through Honora the description of your library, and he (jealous, I am clear, for the magnitude and number of his own library and volumes) set to work at 22 by 34—and there I leave him—till I have *the height* to confound him completely. You see, my dear friends, that you need not again ask me *to go* to see you—for I have seen and I know everything about your home; full as well I know Boston and your home as you know ours at Edgeworthstown. It is your turn now to come and see us again. But I am afraid to invite you, lest you should be disenchanted, and we should lose the delightful gratification we enjoy in your glamor of friendship. Aunt Mary, however, is really all you think and saw her, and in her ninety-first year still a proof as you describe her—and a remarkable proof—of the power of mind over time, suffering and infirmities; and an example of Christian virtues making old age lovely and interesting.

Your prayer, that she might have health and strength to enjoy the gathering of friends round her, has been granted. Honora and her husband, and Fanny and her husband, have all been with us this summer for months; and we have enjoyed ourselves as much as your kind heart could wish. Especially *"that beautiful specimen of a highly-cultivated gentlewoman"* as you so well called Mrs. E., has been blest with the sight of all her children round her, all her living "aughters and their husbands, and her grandchildren. Franci" will settle at home and be a good country gentleman and his own agent—to Mrs. E.'s and all our inexpressible comfort and support, also for the good of the country, as a resident landlord and magistrate *much* needed. As *he* is at home I can be spared from the rent-receiving business, etc., and leaving him with his mother, Aunt Mary and Lucy, I can indulge myself by accepting an often-urged invitation from my two sisters Fanny and Honora, to spend some months with them in London. I have chosen to go at this quiet time of year, as I particularly wish not to encounter the bustle and dissipation and lionizing of London. For tho' I am such a minnikin lion now, and so old, literally without teeth or claws, still there be, that might rattle at the grate to make me get up and come out and stand up to play tricks for them—and this I am not able or inclined to do. I am afraid I should growl—I never could be as good-humored as Sir Walter Scott used to be, when rattled for and made to "come out and stand on his hind legs," as he used to describe it, and then go quietly to sleep again.

I shall use my privilege of seventy-two—rising seventy-three—and shall keep in my comfortable den: I will not go out. "Nobody asked you, ma'am," to play Lion, may perhaps be said or sung to me, and I shall not be sorry nor mortified by not being asked to exhibit, but heartily happy to be with my sisters and their family and family friends—*all* for which I go. Knowing my own mind very well, I speak the mere plain truth. I shall return home to Edgeworthstown before the London *season*, as it is called, commences, *i.e.*, by the end of March or at the very beginning of April.

This is all I have for the present to tell you of my dear self, or of our family doings or plannings. You see I depend *enough* on the sincerity of your curiosity and sympathy, and I thank you in kind for all you have been so affectionately good to tell me of yourselves.

I have been lately reading Thibeaudeau's ten volumes of the History of Napoleon—*Le Consulat et l'Empire*—immediately after having read the life of Washington by Sparks, a book which I think I mentioned to you had been sent to me by an American Jewess of Philadelphia, Miss Gratz. A most valuable present—a most interesting work it is. The comparison between the characters, power, deeds, fortune and fate of Washington and Napoleon continually pressed on my mind as I read their lives; and continually I wished that some modern Plutarch with more of religious, if not more of moral and political knowledge and philosophy than the ancient times afforded, would draw a parallel—no, not a *parallel*, for that could not be—but a comparison between Napoleon and Washington. It would give in the result a comparison between moral and intellectual power on the highest scale, and with the fullest display in which they have ever been seen in two national heroes. The superior, the universal abilities of Bonaparte, his power of perseverance, of transition of resource, of comprehensiveness, of adaptation of means to ends, and all tending to his own aggrandizement, and his appetite for dominion growing with what it fed upon, have altogether been most astonishingly displayed in the Frenchman's history of Napoleon. The integrity, disinterestedness, discretion, persevering adherence to one great purpose, marking the character and the career of Washington, are all faithfully portrayed by his American biographer, and confirmed by state papers and by the testimony of an independent world. The comparison between what Napoleon and Washington did living, and left dying, of the fruits and consequences of their deeds, would surely be a most striking and useful moral and political lesson on true and false glory, and further, would afford the strongest illustrations of the difference in human affairs of what is called the power of fortune and the influence of *prestige*, and the power of moral character and virtue. See Napoleon deserted at his utmost need by those his *prosperous* bounty gorged. See Napoleon forced to abdicate his twice-snatched imperial sceptre!—and compare this with your Washington laying down his dictatorship, his absolute dominion, *voluntarily*, the moment he had accomplished his great purpose of making his beloved country, the

New World, free and independent. Then the deep, silent attachment shown to him when he retired from the army, parted from military power, took leave of public life, is most touching—quite sublime in its truth and simplicity, in as strong contrast as possible with all the French acclamations, inconstancy, frivolity, desertion, treachery, insult, toward their prostrate idol of an Emperor. I felt while I read, and I feel while I reflect, how much of the difference between Napoleon and Washington must be ascribed to the different times, nations, circumstances in which they were placed. But independent of all these, the comparison ably and clearly drawn would lie between the individual characters—between moral and religious power and influence, and intellectual powers even supported by military glory and political despotism. The comparison would ultimately lie between success and merit, and between their transient and durable effects—their worldly and never-dying consequences.

Forgive me, my dear Mrs. Ticknor, for my having been actually run away with thus, and forgetting what I was going to say when I began. I was going to say that I wish Mr. Ticknor would draw the comparison between these two heroes of false and true glory—between real patriotism, true and great to the last, and ambition using patriotism as a mask, and having it struck from his hand powerless at the last. There is no one more able, better fitted to draw this than your husband. Channing has said well of the character of Napoleon as far as he went. But Mr. Ticknor, I conceive, has wider views, more means of information, and a less rhetorical style than Channing: and Sparks, having been the biographer of Washington, might be considered as a party too much concerned to be quite impartial. I am ashamed to have written so much that must seem common-place to him. But I will not tear the pages, as I am tempted to do, because there Is a possibility that when you read them to him it might turn his mind to the subject—and no matter for the rest.

*   *   *   *   *   *   *

I do not know whether I was most interested, dear Mrs. Ticknor, in your picture of your domestic life and happy house and home, or by the view you gave me of your public festivity and celebration of your American day of days—your national festival in honor of your Declaration of Independence.

It was never, I suppose, more joyously, innocently and advantageously held than on the day you describe so delightfully with the accuracy of an eye-witness. I think I too have seen all this, and thank you for showing it to me. It is a picture that will never leave the memory of my heart. I only wish that we could ever hope to have in Ireland any occasion or possibility of such happy and peaceable meetings, with united sympathy and for the keeping alive a feeling of national patriotism. No such point of union *can* be found, alas! In Ireland—no subject upon which sects and parties could coalesce for one hour, or join in rejoicing or feeling for their country. Father Mathew, one might have hoped, considering the good he has effected for all Ireland, and considering his own unimpeachable character and his real liberality, admitting all sects and all parties to take his pledge and share his benevolent efforts, *might* have formed a central point round which all might gather. But no such hope! for as I am *just now assured*, his very Christian charity and liberality are complained of by his Catholic brethren, priests and laity, who now begin to abuse him for giving the pledge to PROTESTANTS and say, "What good our fastings, our temperance, our being of the true faith, if Father Mathew treats *heretics all as one*, as Catholics themselves! And would have 'em saved in this world and the next too?" Then I would not doubt but at the last he'd *turn tail!* Aye, turn Protestant himself ENTIRELY. I have written so much to Mr. Ticknor about Father Mathew that I must here stop, or take care lest I run on with him again. Once set a-running, you see how I go on. You having encouraged me, and I from having conversed with you even for a few days, we have so much knowledge of each other's minds that it is as easy and pleasant to me to write as to speak to you. I will send you some Irish tales newly published by Mrs. Hall, which I think you will like, both from their being well-written and interesting portraitures of Irish life and manners, and from the conciliating, amiable and truly *feminine* (not meaning *feeble*) tone in which they are written.

*   *   *   *   *   *   *

I have not yet thanked you enough, I feel, for *Rollo*. Our children all, and we ourselves, delight in him at play and at work, and every way, and we wish to see more of him. If there be any more of him, pray pack him up bag and baggage and send him off by first steamer, steam-haste. By the by, are you or your children acquainted with the elephant who in his haste forgot to pack up his trunk?

If you are not acquainted with him, I shall have the pleasure of introducing him to you and yours.

Meantime, if you wish to be amused, and with what is new and what is true, read Mrs. Wilmot's *Memoirs of the Princess Dashkoff*, and her own residence in Russia. We know enough of the author to warrant the whole to be true. I do not say that she tells the whole truth, but that all she does tell is true, and what she does not tell she was bound in honor and friendship, and by the tacit, inviolable compact between confidence shown and accepted, never to reveal, much less to publish. Both in the Princess Dashkoff's own memoirs (very able and curious) and in Mrs. Wilmot's continuation (very amusing and new) there are from time to time great gaps, on coming to which the reader cries *Ha! Ha!* And feels that he must skip over. These gaps are never covered over; and when we come even to dangerous ground we see that we must not turn that way, or hope to get on in utter darkness and our guide deserting— or, if not *deserting*, standing stock still, obstinately dumb. These memoirs are not a book on which history could absolutely be founded, but a book to which the judicious historian might safely *refer illustrations*, and even for materials, all which it affords being sound and solid. Much more, in short, may these memoirs be depended upon than any or many of the French varnished and vamped-up *Memoires pour servir à l'Histoire*.

After reading the book I wrote to Mrs. Wilmot, and after homage due to her talents and her truth, I ventured to express, what I am sure you will feel if you read the volume, some horror, towards the close, at the Princess Dashkoff's accepting for herself or her sister, or for whoever it was, a ball from Orloff, the murderer—that Orloff who with his own hand strangled his Emperor.

Mrs. Wilmot made me but a lame apology for her dear princess, I think, and an odd answer for herself. In the first place, she said, it was so long ago. As if such a murder could be a by-gone tale! Or as if thirty or forty or any number of years could purify or cleanse a murderer in the eyes and sense of humanity or justice! In the next place she pleaded that she was so much pleased by Orloff's angel daughter who stood beside him, and then with his parental delight in her beauty, simplicity and elegance in the dance.

Mrs. Wilmot was sure I should have felt as she did, and have forgotten the murderer in the father. But, on the contrary, I am afraid I should have forgotten the father in the murderer; I fear I should have seen only "*the vile spot*" which would never *out* of that hand! And oh! That horrible knee—I see it pressing on the body of the breathless Peter; and, through all the music of the ball-room band, methinks I hear "shrieks of an agonizing king."

Possibly in Russia "murder is lawful made by the excess," and may be palliated by the impartial historian's observing, "*It was then necessary that the Emperor should* CEASE TO BE"—soft synonym for assassination.

I ought not to leave Mrs. Wilmot and the Princess Dashkoff, however this may be, with a tragical and unmerited impression on your mind. I am quite convinced the princess had nothing to do with this horrid affair, or that our countrywoman never would have gone or never would have staid with her.

I can also assure you that when you read these memoirs you will be convinced, as I am, that the Princess Dashkoff was quite pure from all the Empress Catherine's libertine intrigues (I can use no softer phrase). This is proved by facts, not words, for no word does she say on the subject. But the fact is that during Orloff, the favorite Orloff's reign and his numerous successors, the Princess Dashkoff was never at court, banished herself on her travels or at her far-distant *territories*; she over-rated, idolized Catharine, but was her real friend, not flatterer.

It is scarcely worth telling you, but I will for your diversion mention that I asked Mrs. Wilmot whether the Princess Dashkoff evermore went about in the costume, which she described, of a man's great-coat, with stars and strings over it, at *the ball*, and with the sentimental old souvenir silk handkerchief about her throat. Yes. But Mrs. Wilmot would not let me laugh at her friend, and I liked her all the better. She defended the oddity by the kindness of the motive. It was not affectation of singularity, but privilege of originality, that should be allowed to a being so feeling and so educated by circumstances and so isolated—so let the ragged handkerchief and the old gloves museumized pass, and even the old overall of the man's coat on a woman and a princess—so be it.

But from the time of Cardinal Chigi and his one stump of a twenty-years-old pen on which he piqued himself, I quite agree with Cardinal Mazarin[11] that these petty singularities are proofs of a little mind, instead of an originality of genius.

And now, my dear Mrs. Ticknor, "Bisogna levar l'incommodità"—to use the parting phrase of a vulgar Italian who feels that she has made an unconscionable visit: or, as the cockney would say as she got up to depart from a morning *visitation*, "Time for me to be going, I think." And if you do not think so, or have not thought so ten pages ago, you are more indulgent and fonder of me than I had any right or reason to expect, even after all I have heard *from* and seen *of* you.

I promise you that you shall not be so tried again for a twelvemonth to come, at the least. Give my kind remembrances to your eldest daughter, who so kindly remembers me, and give a kiss for me to your youngest, that dear little plaything who cannot remember me, but whom I shall never forget; nor her father's fond look at her, when the tear was forgotten as soon as shed.

Ever affectionately, dear Mrs. Ticknor,

Your obliged friend,

MARIA EDGEWORTH.

Turn over, and as the children's fairy-boards say, "you shall see what you shall see."

N. B.—Among the various scratchifications and scarifications in this volume, you may remark that there have been reiterated scratches at Mrs. and Miss Wilmot, and attempts alternately to turn the lady into *Mrs.* and Miss.

Be it now declared and understood that the lady is not either Mrs. or Miss Wilmot, but Mrs. Bradford—born *Wilmot*, daughter of a Mr. and Mrs. Wilmot of Cork—went over to Russia to *better herself* at the invitation of the Princess Dashkoff, who had, in a visit to Ireland, become acquainted with some of her family. What motives induced her to go to Russia, except the general notion of bettering her fortune, I cannot tell. But she did better her fortune, for the princess gave her pearls in strings, and diamonds in necklaces and rings, and five thousand solid pounds in her pocket, for all which she had like to have been poisoned before she could clear away with them out of Russia.

When she came back she married, or was married to, Mr. Bradford, a clergyman, and now lives in Sussex, England.

Now, in consideration of my having further bored you with all this, be pleased whenever you see *Mrs.* or *Miss Wilmot* in the foregoing pages to read *Mrs. Bradford*, and you will save me thereby the trouble and danger of scratching Mrs. or Miss Wilmot into ten or eleven holes.

The visit to London referred to was paid. Part of the time was spent agreeably visiting friends, seeing sights and reading new books, among them Darwin's *Voyage in the Beagle*, which delighted Miss Edgeworth. But the larger portion of her stay was occupied in nursing her sister Fanny through a weary illness, with the added mental anxiety of knowing that Mrs. Edgeworth was ill at home. Both invalids, however, happily recovered, yet Miss Edgeworth was to find an empty chair on her return; her aunt, Mary Sneyd, had been taken away at the advanced age of ninety. As often before, she felt the sorrow keenly, but rallied bravely from its effects for the sake of those who were left and who depended on her yet more.

During the summer of 1842 Mr. and Mrs. S. C. Hall visited Ireland. They spent some days at Edgeworthstown, with the avowed purpose of writing of its occupants, and we have from their pen also a pleasant picture of the family home-life:—

"The library at Edgeworthstown" (say the writers) "is by no means the reserved and solitary room that libraries are in general. It is large and spacious and lofty; well stored with books, and embellished with those most valuable of all classes of prints—the suggestive; it is also picturesque, having been added to so as to increase its breadth; the addition is supported by square pillars, and the beautiful lawn seen through the windows, embellished and varied by clumps of trees judiciously planted, imparts much cheerfulness to the exterior. An oblong table in the centre is a sort of rallying-point for the family, who group around it, reading, writing or working; while Miss Edgeworth, only anxious upon one point—that all in the house should do exactly as they like, without reference to her—sits quietly and abstractedly in her own peculiar corner on the sofa, her desk—upon which lies Sir Walter Scott's pen, given to her by him when in Ireland—placed before her upon a little quaint table, as unassuming as possible. Miss Edgeworth's abstractedness would puzzle the philosophers: in that same corner, and upon that table, she has written nearly all that has enlightened and delighted the world. There she writes as eloquently as ever, wrapt up to all appearance in her subject, yet knowing, by a sort of instinct, when she is really wanted in dialogue; and, without laying down her pen, hardly looking up from her page, she will, by a judicious sentence wisely and kindly spoken, explain and elucidate in a few words, so as to clear up any difficulty; or turn the conversation into a new and more pleasing current. She has the most harmonious way of throwing in explanations—informing without embarrassing. A very large family party assemble daily in this charming room, young and old bound alike to the spot by the strong cords of memory and love. Mr. Francis Edgeworth, the youngest son of the present Mrs. Edgeworth, and of course Miss Edgeworth's youngest brother, has a family of little ones who seem to enjoy the freedom of the library as much as their elders. To set these little people right if they are wrong; to rise from her table to fetch them a toy, or even to save a servant a journey; to mount the steps and find a volume that escapes all eyes but her own, and, having done so, to find exactly the passage wanted—are hourly employments of this most unspoiled and admirable woman. She will then resume her pen, and, what is more extraordinary, hardly seem to have even frayed the thread of her ideas; her mind is so rightly balanced, everything is so honestly weighed, that she suffers no inconvenience from what would disturb and distract an ordinary writer."

Miss Edgeworth wrote of this notice:—

Mrs. Hall has sent to me her last number, in which she gives Edgeworthstown. All the world here are pleased with it, and so am I. I like the way in which she has mentioned my father particularly. There is an evident kindness of heart and care to avoid everything that could hurt any of our feelings, and at the same time a warmth of affectionate feeling, unaffectedly expressed, that we all like in spite of our dislike to that sort of thing.

Early in 1843 Miss Edgeworth was taken seriously ill with bilious fever, from the effects of which she recovered but slowly. In late autumn she once more went to London to pass the winter with her sister. It was to be her last visit. She enjoyed it with all the freshness of youth, sight-seeing and visiting without fatigue, even attending an opening of Parliament, which she protested had not tired her more than if she had been eighteen. Her prayer and hope was, as it had been her father's, that her body might not survive her mind, and that she might leave a tender and not unpleasing recollection of herself in the hearts of her friends. Her letters certainly showed no falling-off in power, as is amply proved by one written during this visit to her Boston friends:—

LONDON, 1 North Audley street,
Grosvenor square, January 1, 1844. }

MY DEAR FRIENDS MR. AND MRS. TICKNOR:

I cannot begin this new year better, or more to my own heartfelt satisfaction, than by greeting you with my best wishes for many, many happy years to you of your domestic felicity and public estimation—*estimation* superior to celebrity, you know, Mr. Ticknor, disdaining *notoriety*, which all low minds run after and all high minds despise. How I see this every day in this London world, and *hear* it from all other worlds—loudly from your New World across the great Atlantic, where those who make their boast of independence and equality are struggling and quarreling for petty preëminence and "vile trash."

I have been here with my sister, Mrs. Wilson, in a peaceful, happy home these six weeks, and the rattle of Grosvenor square, at the corner of which her house is, never disturbs the quiet of her little library, which is at the back of the house, and looks out upon gardens and trees (such as they are!)....

Among the pleasantest days I have enjoyed in London society, among friends of old standing and acquaintance of distinguished talents, I spent two days at my very good old friend Dr. Holland's, where I heard your name and your letter to your countrymen on Sydney Smith's memorial spoken of in the highest terms of just estimation! You know that Dr. Holland is married to Sydney Smith's daughter. I hope you know Dr. Holland's book, *Medical Notes*, which, though the title might seem exclusively professional, is full of such general and profound views of the human mind as well as body, that it could not but be interesting to you, and would prove to you for my present purpose that he is a person whose estimation and whose praise is worthy of you....

I do not know whether you made acquaintance, when you were in London, with Sydney Smith's brother, Mr. Robert S., or, as he is strangely cognomened (or nicknamed) Bobus Smith. He is well known as one of the celebrities of Holland House, where he has been figuring this half-century. But he no longer figures as a diner-out, and indeed, I believe from that notoriety he always seceded. He is now old and blind, but nevertheless has a most intelligent, energetic countenance, and I should almost say penetrating eye. When he turns and seems to look at me, I feel as if he looked into my face, and am glad so to feel, as he encourages me to open my mind to him by opening his own at once to me. I saw him for the first time a few evenings ago at Dr. Holland's, and sat between him and your American ambassador,

Mr. Everett. I was much pleased by their manner towards each other, and by all they said of the letter of which I spoke. Mr. R. Smith has, in the opinion of all who know him and his brother, the strongest and highest and deepest powers of the two; not so much wit, but a more sound, logical understanding—superior might in the reasoning faculty. If the two brothers' hands grasped and grappled for mastery, with elbows set down upon the table, in the fashion in which schoolboys and others try strength, Robert Smith's hand would be uppermost, and Sydney must give way, *laughing* perhaps, and pretending that he only gave way to fight another day. But independently of victory or trials of strength, the earnestness for truth of the blind brother would decide my interest and sympathy in his favor.

Mr. Everett and Mr. R. Smith seemed to me properly to esteem each other, and to speak with perfect courtesy and discretion upon the most delicate national questions, on which, in truth, they liberally agreed more than could have been or was expected by the bystanders of different parties. Oh, Party Spirit! Party Spirit! How many follies, how many outrages are committed in thy name, even in common conversation!

Mr. Everett did me the honor to come to visit us a few mornings after I had first met him at Dr. Holland's, and sat a good hour conversing as if we had been long known to each other. It is to me the most gratifying proof of esteem to be thus let at once into the real mind, the *sanctum sanctorum*, instead of being kept with ceremonials and compliments on the steps, in the ante-chamber, or even in the *salle de reception*, doing *Kotoo* Chinese or any other fashion.

We went over vast fields of thought in our short hour, from America to France, and to England and to Ireland, Washington, Lafayette, Bonaparte, O'Connell. You may guess it could only be a *vue d'oiseau*, flying too, but still a pounce down upon a true point now and then, and agreeing in our general unchangeable view that moral excellence is essential to make the man really great; that the highest intellectual superiority that can be given by Omnipotence to mortal ought not and does not, even in human opinion, entitle him without moral worth to the character of great. Mr. Everett tells me that Washington Irving is going to publish another life of Washington. I fear his workmanship will be too fine and delicate for the main matter. Boldness, boldness, boldness—and brevity. Oh, the strength of brevity! Brevity keeps fast hold of the memory, and more fast hold of the judgment; the whole process, *en petit compris*, goes in a few words with the verdict to "*long posterity*," while elegance only charms the taste, accords with the present fashion of literature, and passes away, gliding gracefully into "mere oblivion."

Lecture upon brevity well exemplified by present correspondent.

A severe attack of erysipelas laid her low this summer; but if it weakened her body it did not depress her mental faculties. She writes to her cousin with all the buoyancy of youth:—

I am right glad to look forward to the hope of seeing you again, and talking all manner of nonsense and sense, and laughing myself and making you laugh, as I used to do, though I am six years beyond the allotted age and have had so many attacks of illness within the last two years; but I am, as Bess Fitzherbert and poor dear Sophy used to say, like one of those pith puppets that you knock down in vain; they always start up the same as ever.... Sir Henry Marsh managed me with skill, and let me recover slowly, as nature requires at advanced age. I am obliged to repeat myself, "advanced age," because really and truly neither my spirits nor my powers of locomotion and facility of running up and down stairs would put me in mind of it. I do not find either my love for my friends or my love of literature in the least failing. I enjoyed, even when flattest in my bed, hearing Harriet Butler reading to me till eleven o'clock at night.

Her interest in the current literature was sustained; and though she had little sympathy with the romantic school of poetry and fiction that had arisen, her criticisms were both fair and acute. Of the modern French writers she said:—

All the fashionable French novelists will soon be reduced to advertising for a *new vice*, instead of, like the Roman Emperor, simply for a new pleasure. It seems to me with the Parisian novelists a first principle now that there is no pleasure without vice, and no vice without pleasure, but that the Old World vices having been exhausted, they must strain their genius to invent new; and so they do, in the most wonderful and approved bad manner, if I may judge from the few specimens I have looked at.

Henrietta Temple she condemns as "trash," "morally proving that who does wrong should be rewarded with love and fortune." Indeed, so eager was she over books, so ardently did she still enter into all adventures and details, that when she was ill her doctor found it needful to prescribe that her reading must be confined to some old, well-known work, or else something that should entertain and interest her without over-exciting her or straining her attention.

During the whole of 1846 the long illness and death of her brother Francis absorbed all Miss Edgeworth's interest. Next year came the terrible potato famine. She strained every nerve to help the sufferers; her time, her thoughts, her purse, her whole strength, were devoted to the poor. She could hardly feel or think on any other theme; plans to relieve the distress, petitions for aid, filled her letters. She even turned her attention once more to writing, in order to get more money for her starving countrymen. The result was

Orlandino, a tale for children, relating the fortunes and reformation of a graceless truant. It was the last work she published—her literary career thus ending, as it began, with a tale to give gladness to childhood. She had her reward in a great pleasure that came to her from America. The children of Boston, hearing what pains their kind friend in Ireland was taking for her unhappy compatriots, as a recognition of their love for her and her writings, organized a subscription. At the end of a few weeks they were able to send her one hundred and fifty barrels of flour and rice. They came with the simple address, worth more to her than many phrases: "To Miss Edgeworth, for her poor."

She was deeply touched and grateful. It touched her also that the porters, who carried the grain down to the shore, refused to be paid; and with her own hands she knitted a woolen comforter for each man and sent them to a friend for distribution. Before they reached their destination the hands that had worked them were cold, and the beating of that warm, kind heart stilled forever.

For scarcely was the famine over, and before Miss Edgeworth's over-taxed strength had time to recoup, another and yet heavier blow was to befall her. Indeed, many deaths and sorrows as she had known, in some respects this was the severest that had for some years come upon her. It was natural to see the old go before her, but not so the young, and when in 1848 her favorite sister Fanny died rather suddenly, Miss Edgeworth felt that the dearest living object of her love had gone.

The shock did not apparently tell on her health, as she continued to employ herself with her usual interest and sympathy in all the weal and woe of her family and many friends, but the life-spring had snapped, unknown perhaps even to her, certainly unknown to those around her. For she bore up bravely, cheerfully, and was to all appearances as bright as ever. Next to doing good, reading was still her greatest pleasure:—

Our pleasures in literature do not, I think, decline with age. Last 1st of January was my eighty-second birthday, and I think that I had as much enjoyment from books as ever I had in my life.

History gave her particular delight:—

I am surprised to find how much more history interests me now than when I was young, and how much more I am now interested in the same events recorded, and their causes and consequences shown, in this history of the French Revolution, and in all the history of Europe during the last quarter of a century, than I was when the news came fresh and fresh in the newspapers. I do not think I had sense enough to take in the relations and proportions of the events. It was like moving a magnifying glass over the parts of a beetle, and not taking in the whole.

Macaulay's history charmed her, and in all her first enthusiasm she wrote a long letter about it to her old friend, Sir Henry Holland. He showed it to Macaulay, who was so struck with its discrimination and ability that he begged to be allowed to keep it. Among all the incidents connected with the publication of his book, nothing, it is said, pleased Macaulay more than the gratification he had contrived to give Miss Edgeworth as a small return for the enjoyment Ih, during more than forty years, he had derived from her writings:—

TRIM, April 2nd, 1849.

MY DEAR DR. HOLLAND:

I have just finished Macaulay's two volumes of the *History of England* with the same feeling that you expressed—regret at coming to the end, and longing for another volume—the most uncommon feeling, I suppose, that readers of two thick octavo volumes of the history of England and of times so well known, or whose story has been so often written, ever experienced. In truth, in the whole course of reading or hearing it read I was sorry to stop and glad to go on. It bears peculiarly well that severe test of being read aloud; it never wearies the ear by the long resounding line, but keeps the attention alive by the energy shown. It is the perfection of style so varied, and yet the same in fitness, in propriety, in perspicuity, in grace, in dignity and eloquence, and, whenever naturally called forth, in that just indignation which makes the historian as well as the poet. If Voltaire says true that "the style is the man," what a man must Macaulay be! But the man is in fact as much more than the style, as the matter is more than the manner. It is astonishing with what ease Macaulay wields, manages, arranges his vast materials collected far and near, and knows their value and proportions so as to give the utmost strength and force and light and life to the whole, and sustains the whole. Such new lights are thrown upon historic facts and historic characters that the old appear new, and that which had been dull becomes bright and entertaining and interesting. Exceedingly interesting he has made history by the happy use and aid of biography and anecdote. A word brings the individual before us, and shows not only his character, but the character of the times, and at once illustrates or condemns to everlasting fame. Macaulay has proved by example how false Madame de Staël's principle was that biography and biographical anecdotes were altogether inadmissible in history—below the dignity or breaking the proportion or unity, I suppose she thought. But whatever might be her reasons, she gave this opinion to Dumont, who told it to me. Much good it did her! How much more interesting historical *précis* in painting or in writing, which is painting in word, are made by the introduction of portraits of celebrated individuals! Either as actors or even as spectators, the bold figures live, and merely by their life further the action and impress the sense of truth and reality. I have pleasure, my dear Dr. Holland, in pointing out to you, warm as it first comes, the admiration which this work has raised to this height in my mind. I know this will give you sympathetic pleasure.

And now, my good friend, in return I require from you prompt and entire belief in an assertion which I am about to make, which may appear to you at first incredible. But try-try; at all events the effort will give you occasion to determine a question which perhaps, excellent metaphysician as you have shown yourself, you never settled whether you can or cannot believe at will.

That which I require you to believe is ☞ that all the admiration I have expressed of Macaulay's work is quite uninfluenced by the self-satisfaction, vanity, pride, surprise, delight, I had in finding my own name in a note!!!!!

Be assured, believe it or not as you may or can, that neither my vanity nor my gratitude weighed with my judgment in the slightest degree in the opinion I formed, or in that warmth with which it was poured out. In fact, I had formed my opinion, and expressed it with no less warmth to my friends round me, reading the book to me, before I came to that note; moreover, there was a mixture of shame and twinge of pain with the pleasure, the pride I felt in having a line in his immortal history given to *me*, when the historian makes no mention of Sir Walter Scott throughout the work, even in places where it seems impossible that genius could resist paying the becoming tribute which genius owes and loves to pay to genius. I cannot conceive how this could be. I cannot bring myself to imagine that the words Tory or Whig, or Dissenter or Churchman, or feeling of party or natural spirit, could bias such a man as Macaulay. Perhaps he reserves himself for the forty-five, and I hope in heaven it is so, and that you will tell me I am very impetuous and prematurely impertinent. Meanwhile, be so good to make my grateful and deeply-felt thanks to the great author for the honor which he has done me. When I was in London some years ago, and when I had the pleasure of meeting Mr. Macaulay, I took the liberty of expressing a wish that he would visit Ireland, and that if he did we might have the honor of seeing him at our house. I am very glad to find that the Battle of the Boyne will bring him here. He must have now so many invitations from those who have the highest inducement to offer, that I hardly dare to repeat my request. But will you, my dear friends, do whatever you can with propriety for us, and say how much Mrs. Edgeworth and myself and our whole family would be gratified by his giving us even a call on his way to some better place, and even an hour of his conversation. I am now at Trim with my sister and dear brother. Trim and its ruins, and the tower, and where kings and generals and poets have been, would perhaps, he may think, be worth his seeing. Dean Butler and my sister feel as I do how many claims Mr. Macaulay must have upon his time in his visit to Ireland; but they desire me to say that if anything should bring him into this neighborhood, they should think themselves highly honored by receiving him. I am sure he would be interested by Mr. Butler's conversation and remarks on various parts of Macaulay's history, and *I* should exceedingly like to hear it commented and discussed. Little *I* must come in, you see, at every close. You will observe that, in speaking of Macaulay's work, I have spoken only of the style, the only point of which I could presume to think my opinion could be of any value. Of the great attributes, of the essential qualities of the historian, accuracy, fidelity, impartiality, I could not, even if I thought myself qualified to judge, attempt to speak in this letter.

But I am sensible that I have neither the knowledge nor the strength, much less the coolness of judgment, necessary to make opinion valuable on such subjects. I could easily give my own opinion, but—of no use. The less I am inclined to speak when I do not know, the more I am anxious to hear; and most delightful and profitable would it be to me to hear the great historian himself speak on many points which I hear discussed by my learned brother, Dean Butler, and others (on Clarendon's character, etc., etc., etc.) We have not yet seen any of the public reviews of Macaulay's history. No doubt the stinging, little, ephemeral insects will come out in swarms to buzz and fly-blow in the sunshine. The warmer, the brighter, the thicker the swarm will be to prick. I hope you will read this unconscionable lengthy letter when you are in your carriage, rolling about from patient to patient, and be patient yourself then, my dear doctor. You are always so very good and kind to me that I encroach. I seldom write such long epistles. As the most impudent beggar-woman in our town says to Mrs. E., "Ma'am, your ladyship, I never beg from any one so much as your ladyship; troth, never from any but you."
...

Give my most kind and affectionate remembrances to Mrs. Holland and your daughters and sons, and

Believe me most garrulously and sincerely yours,

MARIA EDGEWORTH.

This letter, so characteristic in its humility and generous admiration, shows no sign of old age or impaired faculties, neither is there any trace of this in one of the last she ever wrote, addressed to her sister Harriet:—

I am heartily obliged and delighted by your being such a goose and Richard such a gander, as to be frightened out of your wits at my going up the ladder to take off the top of the clock! Know, then, that I am quite worthy of that most unmerited definition of man, "A creature that looks before and after." Before I *let on* to anybody my doubts of my own capability of reaching the na"l on which to hang the top, I called Shaw, and made her stand at the foot of the ladder while I went up, and found I could no more reach the nail than I could reach the moon, Exit Shaw!

Prudence of M. E., Act 2: Summoned Cassidy, and informed him that I was to wind up the clock, and that he was promoted to take off the top for me; and then up I went and wound the clock, and wound it as I had done before you was born, as there is nothing easier, only to see that it is not going to *maintain* at the very instant, which is plainly to be noted by the position of the maintaining pin on the little outer wheel relative to the first deep tooth. You see I am not quite a nincompoop. I send my lines:—

"Ireland, with all thy faults, thy follies too,

I love thee still: still with a candid eye must view

Thy wit too quick, still blundering into sense;

Thy reckless humor; sad improvidence;

And even what sober judges follies call—

I, looking at the heart, forget them all."

MARIA E., May, 1849.

Miss Edgeworth had been staying with Mr. and Mrs. Butler in the spring. When taking leave she was unusually agitated and depressed, but said as she went away: "At Whitsuntide I shall return." On the very day before she was to redeem this promise, she drove out in apparent good health, when a sudden feeling of weakness overcame her and made her return to the house. Severe pains in the region of the heart set in, and after a few hours' illness Maria Edgeworth died—died as she had fondly wished, at home, in the arms of her stepmother. Yet another of her wishes was granted: she had spared her friends the anguish of seeing her suffer from protracted illness. May 22d, 1849, she rose from the banquet of life, where, in her own words, she had been a happy guest.

In her latter years Miss Edgeworth had been asked to furnish prefaces of a biographical character to her novels. She refused, saying she had nothing personal to tell. "As a woman, my life, wholly domestic, cannot afford anything interesting to the public; I am like the 'needy knife-grinder'—I have no story to tell."

Was she right? Or is not the story of so loving and lovable a life worth telling?

FOOTNOTES

[1] It was his habit, and that of his family, to drop all mention of the earlier marriage.

[2] Miss Edgeworth, in her father's Life, states that she was but twelve years old when she returned to Ireland. The date she gives, however, and that afterwards given by her stepmother, show that she must have been sixteen when the removal took place. It can, therefore, have been a mere *lapsus calami* on her part, as this eminently sensible woman was incapable of the silly weakness of concealing her age.

[3] Afterwards changed into *Patronage*.

[4] Afterwards Sir Humphrey Davy.

[5] Miss Edgeworth erroneously, but persistently, speaks of this publication as the *Journal Britannique*.

[6] A contemporary epigram ran thus:—

"La Genlis se consume en efforts superflus,

La vertu n'en veut pas; le vice n'en veut plus."

[7] Afterwards King Louis Philippe. It was at a Swiss school that he taught, not at a German university.

[8] John Langan was the steward; in face and figure the prototype of Thady in *Castle Rackrent*.

[9] It is but fair to add that Bulwer in a note disclaims the excessive severity and sweeping character of this criticism.

[10] She always refused to have her portrait taken, and all published so-called portraits of Maria Edgeworth are purely fancy productions.

[11] This anecdote, attributed by Miss Edgeworth to Mazarin, is told by De Retz, and is to be found in his memoirs.